BERLITZ®

P9-APH-420

TURKEY

1988/1989 Edition

By the staff of Berlitz Guides
A Macmillan Company

How best to use our guide

These 192 pages cover the **highlights of Turkey,** grouped into six regions. Although not exhaustive, our selection of sights will enable you to make the best of your trip.

The **sights to see** are contained between pages 35 and 146. Those most highly recommended are pinpointed by the Berlitz traveller symbol.

The **Where to Go** section on page 32 will help you plan your visit according to the time available.

For **general background** see the sections The Land and the People (p. 8), Facts and Figures (p. 15), History (p. 16) and Historical Landmarks (p. 30).

Entertainment and **activities** (including eating out) are described between pages 147 and 158.

The **practical information,** hints and tips you will need before and during your trip begin on page 160. This section is arranged alphabetically with a list for easy reference.

The **map section** at the back of the book (pp. 182–188) will help you find your way around and locate the principal sights.

Finally, if there is anything you cannot find, look in the complete **index** (pp. 189–192).

2nd Printing 1988/1989 Edition

CONTENTS

The Land and the People		8
Facts and Figures		15
History		16
Historical Landmarks		30
Where to Go		32
Istanbul and Environs		35
	Old Istanbul	37
	Modern Istanbul	56
	Asian Shore	61
	Excursions	62
	Thrace	69
Aegean Coast		73
	Pergamum	73
	Izmir and Environs	74
	Kuşadası and Environs	79
	Bodrum	86
	Marmaris	89
Mediterranean Coast		89
	Fethiye to Phaselis	91
	Antalya to Side	96
	Alanya to Tarsus	102
Central Anatolia		107
	Ankara	108
	Cappadocia	117
	Konya	124
Black Sea Coast		129
	Samsun to Tirebolu	129
	Trabzon	132
	Sumela Monastery	134

CONTENTS

Eastern Turkey		136
	Erzurum	137
	Nemrut Dağı	140
	Van	142
	Mt. Ararat	144
What to Do		147
	Sports	147
	Shopping	149
	Entertainment	153
	Festivities	155
Eating Out		156
Berlitz-Info	Practical Information	160
Maps	West and Central Turkey	182
	Eastern Turkey	184
	Modern Istanbul	185
	Old Istanbul	186
	Ankara	188
Index		189

Cover photo: Istanbul at sunset.

Text:	Nicholas Campbell and Catherine McLeod
Staff Editor:	Barbara Ender
Layout:	Doris Haldemann
Photography:	cover, pp. 20, 23, 32, 36, 37, 40, 43, 45, 53, 55, 57, 60, 61, 63, 67, 71, 78, 79, 80, 83, 86–87, 151, 154, 158, 159 Daniel Vittet;
	pp. 8 (right), 11, 29, 97, 100, 119, 131, 135, 141, 146 Spectrum Colour Library;
	pp. 8 (left), 48, 88, 130 Dominique Michellod;
	pp. 9, 93, 116, 148, 150 Jean-François Ponnaz;
	pp. 13, 17, 110, 113, 143 Claude Huber;
	pp. 24, 75, 104, 138, 144 PRISMA/Schuster GmbH;
	p. 90 PRISMA/Arim;
	p. 105 Tom Brosnahan;
	pp. 121, 122, 127 Françoise Théatre.
Cartography:	Falk-Verlag, Hamburg;
	pp. 6–7, 35, 73, 89, 107, 129, 136 M. Thommen.

Acknowledgements

We would like to thank Muhammet Yoksuç, Ahmet Duru, Atillâ Türker Gökçen, Kâmil Özkan, Remzi Yıldırım and Yüksel Yavuzeş for their help in the preparation of this guide. We are also grateful to the Turkish Ministry of Culture and Tourism for its cooperation—particularly Mrs Zehra Sulupınar in Ankara and Mrs Bilge Tamer in Zurich.

Found an error or an omission in this Berlitz Guide? Or a change or new feature we should know about? Our editor would be happy to hear from you, and a postcard would do. Be sure to include your name and address, since in appreciation for a useful suggestion, we'd like to send you a free travel guide.

Although we make every effort to ensure the accuracy of all the information in this book, changes occur incessantly. We cannot therefore take responsibility for facts, prices, addresses and circumstances in general that are constantly subject to alteration.

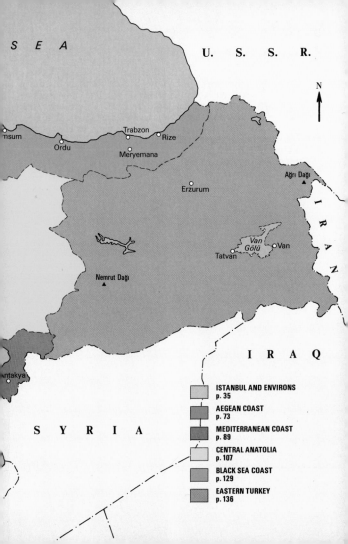

S E A

U. S. S. R.

N

msum

Ordu

Trabzon

Rize

Meryemana

Ağrı Dağı ▲

Erzurum

I
R
A
N

Van
Gölü

Tatvan

Van

Nemrut Dağı ▲

I R A Q

antakya

S Y R I A

ISTANBUL AND ENVIRONS
p. 35

AEGEAN COAST
p. 73

MEDITERRANEAN COAST
p. 89

CENTRAL ANATOLIA
p. 107

BLACK SEA COAST
p. 129

EASTERN TURKEY
p. 136

THE LAND AND THE PEOPLE

Turkey is as intricate and colourful as the pattern of an oriental carpet. Myth and legend, interwoven with the history of six great civilizations, shape the background of this vast land.

Throughout centuries of opulence and decadence, of conquest and defeat, Turkey has been moulded by the conflicting influences of Orient and Occident. Seat of Rome in the East, known as the Byzantine Empire for centuries, it was also the nucleus of the Islamic Ottoman Empire, which at its greatest encompassed Europe as far west as Vienna, together with much of North Africa and the Near East.

Two narrow straits, the Dar-

danelles and the Bosphorus, separate the Asian landmass from Thrace, Turkey's tiny toehold on Europe. At the crossroads of two continents, Istanbul exemplifies Turkey's dual personality. The city teems with life, stippled and confused by the ebb and flow of mighty powers. A walk along a fashionable shopping street, a sophisticated evening in a water-front restaurant will convince you Istanbul is Western. Then see the crowds crossing Galata Bridge, dodge the barrow-men wheeling their carts of cucumbers and tomatoes, penetrate the odiferous bustle of the Spice Market or the calm of a great

All of Turkey in the warmest of smiles and the weirdest of landscapes.

mosque, and you will feel the heartbeat of the Orient.

Istanbul, founded as Byzantium, renamed Nova Roma then Constantinople, was the capital of Turkey until the seat of government was transferred to Ankara in the 1920s. Almost a hundred miles from the nearest coast, and safely out of reach of any enemy warship, Ankara lies in a green oasis in the middle of the dusty Anatolian plain.

Anatolia shares its south-east borders with Syria and Iraq, and stretches to the east to meet Iran and the Soviet Union. The rest of the plain is edged by a fringe of arable land, a verdant coastal strip more than 5,000 miles long. The Black Sea, the Sea of Marmara, the Aegean and the Mediterranean wash Turkey's shores.

The country hoards an unbelievable fund of history. One of the world's oldest cities, Çatalhüyük, was built near Konya almost ten thousand years ago. In the valleys of the Kızılırmak (Red River), the Hittites settled, bringing a class society, a civil code, a powerful monarchy, and the discovery of iron weapons to help keep it that way.

The Hittites were forced back into the mountains in the 17th century B.C., when the "Sea People" came over from Greece and established trading posts around the coast. Other Greeks followed: the Aeolians and Ionians, then the Dorians. They founded a host of illustrious cities—among them Ephesus and Miletus, Aphrodisias and Didyma. And they built Troy.

There, according to Homer's *Iliad,* the great warriors Hector, Achilles and Ajax met their end, and cunning Odysseus devised the wooden horse that terminated the ten-year siege of the city. History attributes the Trojan War to economic causes, but it's a rare visitor who, knee-deep among wild flowers and marble fragments, doesn't call up the image of Helen. Her loveliness put gods and men at odds, launched ships and armies, set Troy burning and laid the neighbouring plain to waste.

The tales of many other heroes hover midway between history and legend. Jason and the Argonauts rowed their way against the treacherous currents of the Bosphorus in search of the Golden Fleece. Everything that Midas touched turned to gold, until he bathed in the Pactolus, near Sardis; Croesus gathered his fabulous wealth by panning the gold from the same river. Alexander the Great won the coastal cities from the Persians, before they passed into Roman hands. St. Paul travelled the southern coast in 47 A.D.

Mystic philosopher Mevlana rests beneath Konya's conical dome.

THE LAND AND THE PEOPLE

As the pivot of the Byzantine Empire, Turkey flourished while the Roman Empire waned in the west. With the help of Crusaders from Europe, it withheld envious attackers until the Ottoman leader Mehmet II took Constantinople in 1453. An era of architectural splendour emerged: Byzantine churches were replaced with mosques bearing huge domes and sleek minarets. The sultans surrounded themselves with beautiful concubines, hidden from the outside world. It's hard to believe, but the last sultan of the Ottoman Empire was still in residence in 1922. Then modern Turkey burst onto the scene.

Throughout the country you will find photographs of the man who made today's Turkey what it is—Mustafa Kemal, later to be known as Atatürk. Unlike the enforced homage in some countries, the Turks are proud to display portraits of Atatürk in homes, shops and restaurants as a genuine and committed sign of their affection.

Atatürk carried out his reforms with characteristic firmness, speed and simplicity. He banned the fez—introduced by the Ottoman sultan Mahmut II a hundred years earlier—by donning a western-style hat and announcing: ''This is the head-gear of civilized people.'' Told it would take seven years to replace

Arabic script with the Latin alphabet, he ordered it to be in use in schools and newspapers within seven weeks. And it was.

Significantly, women remember Atatürk with special devotion, since he raised their status when he came to power. Polygamy was abolished—up to then, men were allowed to have their own private harem of as many as four wives. Divorce by the wife also became possible for

Despite spectacular reforms, many Turkish women still live in a bygone age.

the first time. Women gained the right to vote in national elections, and the first female deputies were elected to parliament.

More than half of Turkey's 51 million inhabitants live in country areas, occupying themselves either with fruit, vegetable and tobacco cultivation or with the vast areas of grassland that produce cereals and ideal grazing for animals. Despite an unemployment figure wavering around the 17 per cent mark, the Turks learn to be resourceful at an early age. Along mountain roads miles from civilization, small children lie in wait for passing cars, then leap out, brandishing plates piled high with fresh-picked strawberries, apricots, figs, cherries, plums or bananas. In the towns, shoe-shine boys from seven to eighty cheerfully polish the grime from your shoes, while their friends coax you onto their borrowed bathroom scales. Others sell sesame-seed rings from huge aluminium trays, fetch tea and coffee for shopkeepers entertaining potential clients, or act as unofficial guides.

Well over 2¼ million Turks—more than 4 per cent of the country's population—emigrate to work or live abroad. The vast majority of them head for West Germany, with the intention of returning after a few years to start a business. It may not help Turkey's confused identity, but it relieves the employment problem and certainly is manna from heaven for the economy.

And Turkey has now found a new source of income: tourism. Not only can it offer beaches, blue waters, a hot climate and an undeniable historical interest, it has a further asset: low prices. To meet the needs of the ever-increasing numbers of summer visitors, resorts are mushrooming all along the Aegean and Mediterranean coasts. Marinas and holiday villages, villas and hotels spring up almost overnight. The Ministry of Culture and Tourism plans to increase accommodation in the two regions, and foreign capital is flowing in steadily. The Black Sea, too,

has its share of beaches, often in placid bays still untouched by the trappings of tourism.

Hotels around the coast serve traditional Turkish fare. Enticing aromas haunt you from street to street: grilled lamb; mackerel or mullet from the morning's catch; the hint of lemon in a cauldron of lamb broth. Venture farther east and a village *lokanta* may have a surprise or two in store. The food will be unpretentious but generally wholesome and very cheap. The waiter, who may be the cook and perhaps also the owner, more than makes up in enthusiasm for anything he lacks in finesse.

Turkish people have an overwhelming interest in their foreign visitors, who are still something of a novelty. Along the roadside, children wave frantically; in towns, knots of passers-by stop to stare, often with the same engaging smile, never with the intention of being rude. If you need directions, a dozen people will clamour to help, offering to speak English or German. They may not understand what you're saying, but don't blame them —it's all part of the friendly spontaneity of the Turk. Hospitality here is no cliché.

And even in 20th-century Turkey, with the harems long closed and the veil no more than a fleeting memory in the wind, the magic of the Orient lingers.

FACTS AND FIGURES

Geography: Turkey covers an area of 779,452 sq. km. (300,948 sq. mi.), the greater part of it in Asia (Anatolia, formerly Asia Minor) and some 3 per cent in Europe (eastern Thrace). The two areas are separated by the Sea of Marmara, which leads east via the Bosphorus Strait to the Black Sea and west via another strait, the Dardanelles, to the Aegean Sea. The country stretches 1,565 km. (972 mi.) from west to east and 650 km. (404 mi.) from north to south. Three-quarters of its frontier is coastal: the Black Sea to the north; the Aegean Sea to the west; and the Mediterranean Sea to the south.

Highest point in the country is Mt. Ararat at 5,165 m. (16,946 ft.). Turkey's longest river, the Kızılırmak, flows 1,355 km. (842 mi.) into the Black Sea. The rivers Tigris (Dicle) and Euphrates (Fırat) start in southeastern Turkey.

Population: 51,421,000, about 56 per cent in rural areas. Major cities: Ankara (capital), 1,878,000; Istanbul, 2,733,000; Izmir, 758,000; Adana, 575,000; Bursa 445,000.

Government: One-chamber parliament, the Grand National Assembly, with 400 deputies voted in for 5-year terms by the public and an executive president chosen by the Assembly for 7 years, not eligible for re-election. A clause in the 1982 Constitution confirmed as head of state the president of the National Security Council, which took power in 1980 following a military coup.

Economy: Emphasis on industry and agriculture, together accounting for just under 50 per cent of Gross National Product. Principal exports: textiles, tobacco, cotton, cereals and pulses, fruit, hazelnuts.

Religion: Approximately 99 per cent of Turks are Muslims, although Islam is not the official religion since Turkey is a secular state.

Language: Turkish. English is widely spoken in resort areas, although in some northern and eastern parts of the country German is better understood.

HISTORY

The Republic of Turkey is young among nations, but the country's history goes back to the dawn of humanity. Three per cent of its present area links it to Europe; the rest lies in Asia, on the Anatolian peninsula, a huge expanse of mountains and plateaus. Turkey's importance as a hinge between east and west is nothing new: it has always played this role, simply because of its situation.

Implements from the Stone Age show that Anatolia was already inhabited in the Middle Palaeolithic Period—between 100,000 and 40,000 B.C. Millennia later, some 5,000 years ago, the Bronze Age originated around the Nile and Tigris and Euphrates. Royal graves have been found in Anatolia containing bronze objects from the 3rd millennium B.C.

About this time the Sumerians of Mesopotamia (the region between the Tigris and the Euphrates in today's Iraq) developed pictographs into a cuneiform (wedge-shaped) script. Some 1,000 years later, Assyrian traders introduced this invention to Anatolia, where the indigenous Hatti people had reached an advanced intellectual level.

The Hittites

Most prosperous of all the Assyrian colonies was ancient Kanesh, today's Kültepe, near Kayseri, one of Turkey's foremost archaeological sites. Tablets from there bear evidence of increasing numbers of Hittite people moving into the area from about 1500 B.C. Their origins remain mysterious (their language was deciphered only in

1915), but they came from the direction of the Caucasus mountains. Two hundred years later they were firmly ensconced.

Hittite domination is divided into three periods: the Old Kingdom (c.1600–1450 B.C.), the New or Empire Period (1450–1200 B.C.) and the Late Hittite Period (1200–700 B.C.). An early capital rose at Hattuşaş (now Boğazköy), north-east of Ankara. Extensive fortifications and temples were erected, as well as a citadel encompassing an impressive library of 3,350 cuneiform tablets built in the 13th century B.C.

Warriors in pixie hats march along the walls of the New Hittite sanctuary near Hattuşaş.

During the momentous Empire Period, an energetic Hittite king, Muwatallis, overcame the forces of the Egyptian pharaoh, Ramses II, at Kadesh in c.1288 B.C. Ramses never conceded defeat; he was too proud for that. He even had obelisks inscribed claiming victory. But he was sufficiently aware of Hittite strength to make terms with the next king, Hattusilis III. Until about 1200 B.C., Hittites and Egyptians wielded comparable and unchallenged power.

The Hittite Empire ended with the arrival of the Phrygians and Achaeans, or "Sea Peoples", who forced the Hittites south into the mountains, where they remained until advancing Assyrians took over, this time to rule and not to trade.

Troy and After

Meanwhile, far away on the Aegean coast, other events had been taking place. The ancient Greeks traditionally recounted their history starting from the fall of Troy. Much clamorous academic discussion surrounds the exact date of the Trojan War, but it is generally thought that Troy was destroyed in 1260 B.C.

Strategically set above the Hellespont, now known as the Dardanelles, nine Troys rose and fell over the centuries. There is no doubt that the Trojan War did occur, although just which of the superimposed layers of ruined cities was the actual site has never been established. Archaeologists hesitate between the levels known as Troy VIIa and Troy VI. In Homer's accounts in the *Iliad* and the *Odyssey*, Troy was a well-organized, wealthy city, governed by the prudent, peace-loving King Priam.

Within a century, the Mycenaean Greeks who conquered Priam's city saw their own civilization decline. A race known as the Dorians either invaded or gained power in southern Greece, motivating many mainlanders to pack up their chattels and families and set forth across the Aegean to the coast of Anatolia. They immigrated in waves. First came the Aeolians, who went to the northern stretch of coastline above old Smyrna, creating a region known as Aeolis; then the Ionians, who settled south between Smyrna and the river Maeander. Smyrna itself started as an Aeolian town, then it became Ionian. Later, the Dorians followed, installing themselves south of the Maeander, in Caria.

Mainland Greece plunged into a dark age of limited achievement. Not so Ionia, where an outstanding culture evolved. Before 800 B.C. the 12 main Ionian cities banded together to form the Pan-Ionic League. Later,

Smyrna was admitted as a 13th member. The arts, science and philosophy thrived. Not that everything was peaceful—the cities continued to squabble among themselves—but their citizens lived well, and many of the settlements founded colonies.

Rich as Croesus

Inland lived the Lydians, powerful and wealthy neighbours who pushed west towards the Aegean coast to set up their capital at Sardis. Croesus, the most famous Lydian king, owed his legendary fortune to gold from the River Pactolus and, according to Greek tradition, invented the first coins of standard shape and weight. Unfortunately for Croesus, his ambitions took him east as well as west, into Persia, where he was roundly defeated. He was driven back to Sardis, only to witness the sacking of his city by Cyrus the Great in 546 B.C.

With Lydia absorbed, the Greek coastal cities lay wide open to the Persians, who lost no time incorporating them into their empire. Ionia attempted rebellion but was easily subdued in 494 B.C. Provoked by Athenian support for the Ionians, the Persian king Darius directed his attention to the Greek mainland. He was defeated at Marathon in 490, and ten years later his son Xerxes lost his fleet at Salamis.

The following year, on the same day, Xerxes' army was defeated at Plataea and his fleet at Mycale. The coastal cities were encouraged to cluster together into the Delian Confederacy, paying tribute to Athens in return for protection against the Persians. Athens grew so attached to this easy source of income that pleas for release from the agreement went unheard. Sparta won the remunerative Confederacy from Athens at the outcome of the Peloponnesian War. The alert Persians, sensing weakness, rushed to the attack, and the Greek cities of the Aegean coast were theirs at last.

Alexander's Dream

A new star was rising on the Greek mainland: Macedon in the far north, whose king, Philip II, aimed at unifying the Greek world. His wildest dreams were fulfilled after his death by his son, Alexander the Great, in a short lifetime of 33 years. In 334 B.C., aged 24, Alexander crossed the Hellespont. He paused to pay homage to the heroes of Troy before taking over the whole Aegean coast. After conquering Syria and Egypt, he overcame Persepolis, the Persian capital, before advancing further still, into India. In 12 years he established some 70 cities across the face of the eastern world. Aristotle's

most brilliant pupil, Alexander dreamed of a world empire. The dream foundered. At his death the conquered territory was divided among various generals, whose antagonism and expansionist lust finally laid their land open to Roman incursions. Some of Alexander's legacy survived, notably the Greek language, which had become the usual medium for business and cultured discussions.

Enter the Romans

Outstanding among coastal cities was Pergamum, governed by the Attalid dynasty. The last Attalid king, Attalus III, has gone down in history as an odd character. One of his hobbies was inventing poisons and testing them on reluctant slaves. Just how eccentric he had become was not clear until his death (from natural causes) in 133 B.C., when Pergamese citizens were dismayed to learn he had bequeathed the whole province to the Romans. Thus Pergamum became capital of the new Roman province they called Asia. Mithradates VI, king of Pontus, tried to resist Roman occupation, going so far as to order the massacre of all Romans in Asia, irrespective

Part of the legacy of ancient Rome: the library of Celsus at Ephesus.

of age, sex or rank. This act of atrocity accounted for 80,000 lives. But the Romans got their revenge: after numerous campaigns, their legions triumphed.

In 27 B.C. Octavian took the title Augustus; Rome ceased to be a republic and became an empire. There followed a long period of calm prosperity known as the *Pax Romana* ("Roman Peace"). All Asia Minor was now incorporated into the Roman Empire. Except for the military bases where Latin was the normal means of communication, coastal citizens still spoke Greek, while Anatolian languages continued among the people who had always used them. The old Greek cities were embellished with grandiose Roman buildings, many the result of private donations.

A new religion was causing problems. Christianity represented a threat because it challenged the sanctity of the official gods and the emperor. The voyages of the Apostle Paul, from A.D. 40 to 56, removed some of the mystery that had made Christianity appear dangerous in the eyes of the establishment. As he journeyed, he set up Christian communities, notably the Asian churches addressed in the Revelation of St. John: Ephesus, Smyrna, Pergamum, Thyatira, Sardis, Philadelphia and Laodicea.

Byzantium the Golden

Byzantium had already developed on the banks of the Bosphorus and the Golden Horn. Legend claims that a Greek, Byzas, arrived in about 660 B.C. to found a settlement in obedience to the Delphic Oracle, which bade him build his city "in front of the blind". When he saw that early settlers were living in present-day Kadiköy on the Asian shore, he presumed they were the "blind", because they had overlooked the supreme appeal of the other, European bank, where he set up his town.

Byzantium, like the coastal cities, had encountered the power of Athens, Sparta, Persia and Alexander the Great. It attempted independence from Rome but was too small to hold out against the new mistress of the world and was conquered by the emperor Septimius Severus in A.D. 196. At first he punished the Byzantians with acts of destruction, then, seduced by the sheer loveliness of the place, he began to build, enlarging and strengthening the old defensive walls.

A succession of inadequate rulers led to the gradual decline of the Roman Empire. In 293 Diocletian thought to strengthen it by dividing it into two parts. He became Emperor of the East, while the West was governed by Maximian. This momentous decision was to have incalculable effects. Byzantium, already renowned, stood as capital of the eastern empire. However, after the abdication of Diocletian and Maximian in 305, the empire continued to weaken, harassed by Germanic tribes. For a time, Constantine and Licinius ruled in harmony, then relations deteriorated. In 324 Constantine, who supported Christianity, defeated his pagan ally and reunited the whole empire. He immediately began construction of a new capital, choosing Byzantium as the site. It was to be known by the name Secunda Roma; soon it became Nova Roma, then Constantinopolis in honour of the emperor. He officially inaugurated his city with tremendous ceremony in 330. Constantine added to the walls, following an outline suggested, he claimed, in a vision of Christ. The circuit included seven hills, in memory of the seven hills of Rome. The emperor died a confessed Christian.

In the Christian world, Constantinople achieved a pre-eminence it was to maintain for 1,000 years after the fall of Rome in 476 to the Germanic tribes.

Glowing Byzantine mosaics in St. Saviour in Chora depict the life and power of Christ.

22

However, the city was constantly under threat of invasion, while subjected internally to endless political and religious wrangling.

The Byzantine or Eastern Roman Empire (476–1453) knew its finest hours in the 6th century under Justinian the Great. His reign produced a laudable legal system, the celebrated Code of Justinian, and saw the empire extend to Spain, Italy and Africa. Creative art was encouraged,

Justinian strengthened the walls of Sumela Monastery when he saw its strategic possibilities.

producing rich, colourful styles in furniture and clothing, and gloriously illuminated manuscripts. As part of a great building programme, the unsurpassed basilica of St. Sophia was constructed.

After the death of the Prophet

24

Muhammad in 632, the tremendous expansion of the Arabs led to the development of the Islamic empire. Syria, Jerusalem and Egypt were rapidly taken from the Byzantines. Constantinople was seriously threatened from 674 to 678; however its walls withstood siege. The Byzantine Empire continued to diminish with the loss of North Africa and Italy, then saw another golden age under Basil I (867–886) who greatly increased military strength. In 1042 Seljuk Turks, who had originated in central Asia, began to drive the Byzantines from Asia Minor, and the Normans won control of Sicily and Naples: the empire was slowly crumbling.

Although the Greek and Roman churches had split, western Christendom stood allegedly on the side of Byzantium when it came to confronting "infidel" races such as the Seljuk Turks. Islamized in the 10th century, the Seljuks were fiercely committed to their new religion. They overran Anatolia, menacing Christian holy places and swooping on pilgrims bound for Jerusalem. The First Crusade was organized to help the Byzantines recapture the Holy Land from the Muslims; it resulted in victory for the crusaders. During the Second and Third crusades, the European Christians suffered overwhelming defeat. The Fourth,

launched in 1202, abetted by Venetian jealousy of Byzantium's merchant prowess, turned against Constantinople. The city which had held out against so many attacks was subjected to mindless pillaging by fellow Christians. The crusaders ruled the city from 1204 until 1261; they called their state Romania, which is sometimes referred to as the Latin Empire. Gold, silver, jewels and works of art were stripped from the monuments.

The Lascarid dynasty in Nicaea (Iznik) across the Bosphorus from Constantinople, a remnant of the Byzantine Empire, helped the shattered city to its feet in 1261. However, the era had reached its end: Constantinople was never the same again.

Mehmet the Conqueror

By the 15th century the Ottoman Turks, whose origins were similar to those of the Seljuks, were in control of the whole of Anatolia except Constantinople, which they coveted and frequently besieged. Nicaea's days had proved numbered. In 1330 it was taken by Orhan, first Ottoman sultan. An Ottoman capital was set up in nearby Bursa, before being moved to Edirne, ancient Adrianople. The Byzantine emperor, Manuel II (1391–1425), tried to stem the tide of events by allowing a Turkish district,

25

mosque and tribunal within his city, and by courting Turkish goodwill with a gift of gold florins; all to no avail. The young Ottoman sultan, Mehmet II, set to work to prevent help coming to a beleaguered Constantinople by blocking the routes into the city. A fortress was erected on the European side of the Bosphorus. Then Mehmet withdrew to Edirne to wait for the spring.

The Byzantines tried to protect the Golden Horn by stretching a huge iron chain across the water. They desperately strengthened the defensive walls which had so often stood them in good stead, and watched fearfully for the inevitable. On the naval side, the Turks neatly sidestepped the ruse of the chain by dragging their ships overland on rollers, before putting them together to form a bridge for the soldiers. On May 29, 1453, the final assault was made. The last Byzantine emperor, Constantine XI, fell in the fighting, and by noon Mehmet had control of the city. His first act was to visit St. Sophia for prayer and to declare it a mosque. After allowing his soldiers three days' pillaging, he restored order, acting with considerable leniency and good sense. Henceforth he was to be known as Fatih (the Conqueror), and his capital was named Istanbul.

Splendour and Decline

Mehmet's empire took in most of Greece and the southern Balkans, as well as Anatolia. Under Selim, grandson of the Conqueror, expansion continued.

The most lustrous period occurred during the reign of Selim's successor, Suleiman the Magnificent (1520–1566), greatest of the sultans, known to his compatriots as the Lawgiver. Ascending the throne at age 25, he ruled for 46 years, the longest reign in Ottoman history, rendered glorious by a flowering of culture which included the building of many superb mosques by his chief architect, the remarkable Sinan.

Suleiman's army captured Belgrade in 1521. Eight years later they entered Austria to besiege Vienna (raising the siege 24 days later), then they took most of Hungary. In 1522 Rhodes fell. Muslim corsairs, including the infamous Barbarossa, helped win a part of the North African coast. By the mid-17th century, the Ottoman Empire had reached its widest limits. And they were wide indeed: the frontier extended from Batumi at the extreme east of the Black Sea, southwards to Basra in present-day Iraq. A ribbon along the Red Sea took in Medina and Mecca. Egypt was in Ottoman hands and so was the whole eastern coast of the Mediterranean, including

Cyprus. Greece was a long-standing possession; Crete had fallen. To the north, the empire's territories included the Crimea and an area around the Sea of Azov. Dissolution was inevitable. The process was long and painful, leaving in its wake many problems which still cause trouble in the Middle East today.

Among internal concerns was insurrection from a corps of soldiers known as the *Yeniçeri* ("new troops") or Janissaries. Originally composed of prisoners of war, they later included boys levied from Christian families and converted to the Muslim faith. Sinan himself was one. Later this type of conscription ceased; more and more the Janissaries were made up of a bunch of adventurers drawn from many races. Hated and feared throughout the land, they attained such a position of strength that they practically ran the sultanate. They were not brought under control until the early part of the 19th century.

The Twilight Years

The year 1821 marked the beginning of the war for Greek independence, finally achieved 11 years later. Attempts at reform within the decaying Ottoman Empire had been left too late. In any case, these reforms, albeit genuine, were interrupted by the Crimean War. By 1876 the government was bankrupt. The ruling sultan, Abdul Hamid II, misinterpreting the spirit of the times, tried to apply absolute rule to a country staggering under a load of debt, with a population of mutually hostile groups.

Abdul Hamid's reforms bore fruit in the end—but not in the way he had anticipated. Young army officers and the professional classes were increasingly interested in Western ideals. European literature was being widely studied. Robert College, an American school, and Galatasaray, the French *lycée* in Istanbul, were providing intelligent boys with new ideas of democracy, while Turkish girls, so long shut off from the world, were exposed to similar thoughts in the American women's college at Arnavutköy. These new intellectuals formed a group known as the Young Turks. At first the movement remained underground. Its centre was Salonica, and it was there ultimately that revolt broke out. In 1909 Abdul Hamid was deposed and replaced by Mehmet V, his brother.

There followed the Balkan Wars in which Turkey lost Macedonia and western Thrace, then World War I with Turkey on the side of the Central Powers. In 1915, in the Gallipoli Campaign, the Turks defeated the Allied attack on the Dardanelles.

At the end of the war, the

Turks had to sign the Treaty of Sèvres, which formally ended the existence of the Ottoman Empire. Greece was given large concessions, Armenia was to be an independent state; the British, French and Italians were granted the right to occupy what was left of the Turkish lands. The subsequent period of internal strife with Greeks and Armenians living in Anatolia, and struggles with occupying Entente powers was dominated by the figure of Mustafa Kemal who, from small beginnings in Macedonia, had risen to become the charismatic leader of Turkish nationalism. In 1920, with the establishment of the Turkish National Assembly, he was elected president and invested with executive power. From 1919 to 1922 he led the Turko-Greek War, which culminated in Greek defeat and withdrawal from Asia Minor. He was then faced with placating the religious elements in his government, while abolishing the sultanate. This meant deposing Sultan Mehmet VI, whose very person stood for the old ideas of combined religious and secular power. The manoeuvre was delicate. Kemal handled it with his usual vigour in a speech to the Assembly: "...it was by force that the sons of Osman seized the sovereignty... now the Turkish nation has rebelled and put a stop to these usurpers."

On November 10, 1922, the sultan, almost bereft of entourage, slipped quietly away from his palace to a waiting British warship. A caliph was appointed as religious leader, with powers strictly limited by Turkish secular law. The office was abolished in 1924.

A Modern State

In 1923 the Treaty of Lausanne defined Turkey's modern sovereignty and borders. Greece and Turkey exchanged their expatriate populations in a movement involving thousands of people.

The decade 1925–1935 witnessed the introduction of resounding reforms. Mustafa Kemal, now usually spoken of as Atatürk (Father of the Turks), set to work secularizing institutions, adapting the Latin alphabet for the Turkish language, emancipating Turkish women, changing the calendar, revising the laws and improving agriculture and industry. He did more than anyone to mould Turkey into a dependable modern nation with a belief in Western democracy. When Atatürk died in 1938, Turks in their thousands lined the track to salute the white presidential train carrying him to Ankara, the new capital.

Turkey remained neutral during World War II. The Democratic Party was elected to power in 1950, staying in position until 1960. The government, faced with ever-increasing economic and social difficulties, was overthrown by the Turkish Army, directed by a National Unity Committee. A new constitution consolidating modernizing reforms was approved by referendum in 1961. Social unrest led to another military coup in September 1980. A new constitution was prepared, and new legislation concerning political parties and elections was drawn up.

In 1982, a democratic form of government was established that has since been working to achieve an industrialized Western-style economy.

Keeping up with the times, many ancient coastal cities have become popular holiday resorts.

29

HISTORICAL LANDMARKS

Prehistory	7000 **B.C.**	First known city established at Çatalhüyük.
	2500	Hatti people inhabit Anatolia.
Hittites	1900	Hittites move in, build capital at Hattuşaş, now Boğazköy.
	1200	Invasion of Achaeans and Phrygians leads to Trojan War. Hittites retreat inland. Hattuşaş falls.
Greeks and Persians	1050	Aeolians, Ionians then Dorians from Greece settle along coast.
	685	Lydian dynasty founded.
	546	Last Lydian ruler Croesus attacks Persians but is defeated by Cyrus the Great. Persians take all Greek cities on Aegean coast.
	334	Alexander the Great conquers Persia and Asia Minor.
	330–130	Great cities flourish: Pergamum, Ephesus. King of Pergamum bequeaths his province to Romans.
Romans	129	Pergamum becomes capital of Asia.
	27	Rome becomes an empire, incorporating the whole of Asia Minor.
	196 **A.D.**	Byzantium, hitherto independent, conquered by Septimius Severus.
	293	Roman Empire divided; Byzantium becomes Roman capital of East.
	324	Constantine reunites empire, rebuilds capital, accepts Christianity.
	330	Capital inaugurated as Constantinople.
	395	Roman Empire permanently divided.

Byzantine Empire	476	Fall of Rome. Eastern Empire survives as Byzantine Empire.
	634	Muslims take over considerable Byzantine territory.
	1042	Seljuk Turks begin to drive Byzantines from Asia Minor. End of Christian kingdom.
	1096	Beginning of Crusades—European Christians sent to fight Seljuks in the Holy Land.
	1204	Crusaders capture Constantinople.
Ottoman Empire	1300	Ottoman Turks rise to power in north-western Asia Minor.
	1453	Constantinople falls to Ottoman Turks under Mehmet II.
	1520–66	Reign of Suleiman the Magnificent.
	1853–56	France and Britain join Ottoman forces against Russia in Crimean War.
	1914–18	Ottoman Empire sides with Germany, Austria-Hungary and Bulgaria during World War I.
	1919–22	Turko-Greek War.
Turkey	1920	Mustafa Kemal sets up provisional government in Ankara.
	1922	Sultanate abolished.
	1923	Republic of Turkey proclaimed. Kemal elected president.
	1938	Death of Kemal Atatürk.
	1960	Military administration takes power, then civilian government restored.
	1980	Political unrest. Military takeover as violence increases.
	1982	New Constitution returns country to civilian administration.

WHERE TO GO

A country more than three times the size of Britain can't be tackled completely in one go. We've split it, therefore, into six regions, each easily manageable on its own: the Istanbul area, taking in the European corner of Turkey and the Sea of Marmara; the Aegean coast; the Mediterranean coast; central Anatolia; the Black Sea coast; and the eastern provinces.

Making a round trip of it is strenuous and only for those with a month or two in which to travel at leisure. But you can visit two or three regions in the course of a normal holiday. All too often, the first, and only, stop is a beach resort on the Aegean or the Mediterranean. It's a pity, since inland Turkey offers such a

lot. So why not do the energetic part first, using Istanbul or Ankara as a base, concentrating on the mosques, museums and archaeological sites, then head for the shore? Judicious planning can get you a hotel close to an ancient coastal city, enabling you to combine a visit with picnic and swimming, probably in the city's original harbour.

Istanbul is a must on any itinerary. Its colourful sprawl can be covered easily by taxi, a cheap way to see the sights. But make sure you also wander at will, soaking in the spell-binding romance of oriental Turkey. A few days in Istanbul will leave you with plenty of time for a cruise along the Bosphorus into the balmy climate of the Black Sea. Alternatively, you can choose a leisurely Aegean voyage to Izmir, if not further down to the Mediterranean.

The Black Sea coast can also be reached from Ankara, traditional base for excursions to the east. The Turkish capital is the natural setting-off point for the very popular triangular trail covering the Hittite cities, the volcanic rock wonderland of Cappadocia and the oldest known remnants of city civilization near Konya. From there, it's only a short hop to the south coast, where the water is warm enough to swim in January. The rugged scenery of the east is best left either to an organized coach tour or to the really adventurous; because of the long distances and the uncertainty of roads and facilities, most people keep to the more accessible areas.

The cheapness and flexibility of air travel helps when it comes to combining regions. The Black Sea port of Trabzon is only an hour from Istanbul, as are the Aegean airport Dalaman and its

33

Mediterranean equivalent, Antalya. Regular services connect Ankara with Erzurum and Van in the east.

Though it may seem the most logical way of seeing the country, driving is not recommended—certainly not if it is your own car. The best that can be said about some of the less frequented roads is that they manage to slow down Turkish drivers. At the same time, they provide regular business for the rows of repair workshops you see occupying entire streets. Even the Ministry of Culture and Tourism warns against using a car anywhere at night.

Not that there's any need to drive, considering the extensive bus service. One of the most unforgettable experiences in Turkey is the *otogar*, the bus station. For sheer bedlam, Istanbul's main intercity terminal is hard to beat. As an obvious passenger, you will be steered through the chaos to a bus that has been waiting only for you to board before leaving. The fare is amazingly cheap, and thrown in for good measure: a tea token, a bottle or two of cold drinking water, several sprinklings of lemon-scented eau de cologne, and a prayer by the driver in the bus station mosque. Whatever is said about the state of Turkish roads and drivers, the bus system is astonishingly efficient, and

generally gets you there faster than a train would.

The golden rule for travellers in Turkey is: relax and take things in your stride. That way you'll view any day-to-day inconveniences as amusing anecdotes rather than serious causes for complaint. The fascination of seeing villagers commuting by donkey and using wooden-wheeled carts that have served since biblical times makes you a privileged spectator to a lost way of life. But you can't have all that and expect five-star comfort all the time. Most important, a willingness to serve is there, and when your host greets you with the words "Hoş geldiniz" (Welcome) he means it. If you can reciprocate with a tentative "Merhaba" (Hello) or "Teşekkür ederim" (Thank you), he'll be delighted.

Finding your way around towns needn't be a problem. Ask for the *turizm büro,* the tourist office. In resort areas, they are well geared to the needs of visitors. Elsewhere, tourist officials often have limited funds but are resourceful enough to provide their own home-made but adequate maps and literature. They also know the area intimately, speak English or have someone on hand who does, and are well qualified to advise you where to stay, where to eat, what to see and how best to get there.

34

ISTANBUL AND ENVIRONS

There will always be something familiar about Istanbul's famous skyline. Curving domes rise in layers, with minarets soaring upwards. In the morning the city seems to drowse behind a gauzy veil, then, progressively, it emerges as the changing light draws endless colours from the buildings. The twilight shades of plum and purple are touched with flashes from spires and windows, while the Bosphorus ripples like heavy silk shot with fire. Istanbul's sunsets are as celebrated as everything else in this old crossroads of history, where, quite literally, east meets west.

Three tremendous civilizations have formed Istanbul: Roman, Byzantine and Ottoman. For a thousand years it was the intellectual centre of the Western world. Today, some 6 million people, the estimated population of Greater Istanbul, are rapidly changing the face of their metropolis. Gardens have been replaced by high-rise buildings, vine-laden alleys are giving way to office blocks, and the wooden houses, which used to lean companionably together in the older quarters, are becoming rare. So, too, are their grander cousins, the summer palaces which once graced the shores of the Bosphorus. Fortunately, the drift has been caught in time. Mystery and charm survive.

For sightseeing purposes, Istanbul can easily be divided into three sections. In Europe, the Old City stretches from Seraglio Point *(Sarayburnu)* to the Theodosian Walls, south of the Golden Horn, while the modern town, Beyoğlu, spreads up the hills north of the waterway. This is the commercial quarter and the main hotel and shopping district. On the Asian bank of the Bosphorus, Scutari *(Üsküdar)* is mainly a residential area.

In the Old City, the major sights can easily and enjoyably be reached on foot. It's probably best to select individually from the remaining monuments on the southern shore of the Golden Horn and use transport to visit them. There are plenty of buses and communal taxis *(dolmuş)*; ordinary taxis are metered and fairly inexpensive. Note that most of Istanbul's museums are closed on Mondays, and some on other days as well. Check with the tourist office before you go.

You'll certainly want to take a boat trip along the Bosphorus, zigzagging from one palace, fortress or little town to another, almost as far as the Black Sea. Dolmabahçe Palace, Yıldız Park and Rumeli Hisarı are all situated along the European shore of the Bosphorus. The Asian shore is the site of Beylerbeyi Palace, Çamlıca Park and Anadolu Hisarı. You can make a similar excursion along the Golden Horn to Eyüp, one of the holiest places in the Muslim world. The Princes Islands in the Sea of Marmara are also interesting to visit. Normal ferries serve all these places.

Further afield, and requiring an overnight stay, the old Ottoman capitals Bursa and Edirne are each worth a trip from Istanbul, as are the war graves of Gallipoli and the ancient ruins of Troy.

OLD ISTANBUL

If you are staying in the hotel district, you will have to cross Galata Bridge to reach the Old City. From the bridge you catch a glimpse of the Asian shore and Leander's Tower, a lighthouse sitting off the coast in the Sea of Marmara. The New Mosque stands in a square where the bridge ends. To the right you can see the imposing mass of the Mosque of Suleiman the Magnif-

A peaceful outlook over the Blue Mosque and the Bosphorus.

icent, seemingly etched against the hillside. In the opposite direction are the roofs of Topkapı Palace and the dome of St. Sophia, which will prove invaluable landmarks, as will the six minarets of the Blue Mosque, needling upwards beside the vast, open area of the Hippodrome.

37

Sultanahmet District

The spacious At Meydanı ("Square of Horses") gives only a faint idea of the magnificence of the **Hippodrome** in Byzantine times, when it was central to the city's life. Inspired by the Circus Maximus in Rome, it was designed as a stadium for chariot racing and public activities. First built in 203, and enlarged by Constantine the Great, the Hippodrome finally attained tremendous dimensions—approximately 400 metres long by 120 across (1,300 by 400 ft.)—and provided seating for 100,000 people.

The Hippodrome was the scene of the official ceremony founding the city of New Rome in 330. Today, few signs remain of past pageantry, for the Hippodrome was destroyed during the Fourth Crusade and gradually stripped of everything, even its marble seats. Statues were melted down for coins. In the 17th century the ruins were quarried to help build the Blue Mosque.

The entrance to the central axis, or *spina*, is marked by a fountain in a helmet-shaped edifice with an ornate gilt and mosaic ceiling, given by Kaiser Wilhelm II to mark his visit to the city in 1900. Three ancient monuments survive along the *spina* itself.

The **Egyptian Obelisk** was commissioned by Thutmose III (1549–1503 B.C.). Brought here in A.D. 390 by the Emperor Theodosius, this is only the top of the original column. Perfectly preserved hieroglyphics inscribed on the smooth pink granite record that Thutmose raised the monument in honour of the Egyptian sun god, Amon Re, and to commemorate his own military conquests. Bas-reliefs on the Byzantine base depict Theodosius and his family in different scenes.

The **Serpentine Column**, originally in the form of three bronze snakes wound together to support a gold vase, is the oldest Greek monument in Istanbul. Constantine the Great brought it from Delphi, where it commemorated the Greek victory over the Persians at Plataea in 479 B.C.

A second obelisk, of indeterminate date, is known as the **Column of Constantine Porphyrogenitus**, because a Greek inscription on its base records that the Emperor Constantine VII Porphyrogenitus (913–959) restored and covered it with gilded bronze plates.

On the western side of the Hippodrome, don't miss the **Turkish and Islamic Arts Museum** (*Türk ve İslam Eserleri Müzesi*). The collection is housed in **İbrahim Paşa Sarayı**, the palace of Suleiman's son-in-law. Apart from superlative illuminated Korans, Turkish and Persian miniatures, carpets and faïence, you'll also see utilitarian objects, giving insight into Turko-Islamic life from the 8th century to the present day.

Blue Mosque

Known in Turkish as *Sultan Ahmet Camii*, this graceful mosque lends its name to the whole surrounding district. It was designed in the early 17th century by the architect Mehmet Ağa.

The mosque rises from the ground in sensuously undulating domes and half-domes, with six slender minarets shooting skywards.

Inside, everything seems to float in the azure light reflected from the blue tiles which give the mosque its name. There are 21,043 ceramic tiles from the town of Iznik, celebrated for the tile industry since the mid-15th century. Lilies, carnations, tulips and roses bloom in ageless, stylized beauty, glowing in the light falling from 260 windows. Until the 18th century they contained stained glass, enhancing the cerulean hues of the interior.

Four massive fluted pillars support a central cupola of gigantic proportions: 22.4 metres (70 ft.) in diameter and 43 metres (142 ft.) at the highest point.

The *mihrab*, or niche, placed in all mosques to show the direction of Mecca, is white marble, and so is the delicately chiselled pulpit. Inlay of mother-of-pearl and ivory enhances the ebony shutters. Painted arabesques around the upper windows are restorations, but if you step under the sultan's loge, you'll see the original decoration of marvellously swirling tendrils executed in jewel-like colours.

Before you visit St. Sophia opposite, it is worth making a short diversion to the nearby **Mosque of Sokullu Mehmet Pasha** *(Mehmet Paşa Camii),* one of the masterpieces of the greatest of all Ottoman architects, Sinan. A further example of original painted decoration, above the entrance, and fine Iznik tiles contribute to its charms.

Further downhill, towards the Sea of Marmara, stands the Byzantine church of Sts. Sergius and Bacchus, known to the Turks as **Küçük Ayasofya Camii** ("Little St. Sophia Mosque"). Some of the lacy capitals in this 6th-century building carry monograms of Justinian and his wife, Theodora, and there is a carved inscription in the gallery mentioning the royal couple and St. Sergius.

St. Sophia *(Ayasofya)*

Opposite the Blue Mosque lies the former church of St. Sophia, undisputed sovereign of Istanbul's First Hill. Constantine the

Great is reputed to have built a basilica here in 325 on the site of a pagan temple. Destroyed twice by fire, it was rebuilt from 532 to 537 by the Emperor Justinian, who dedicated it to the Holy Wisdom of God (in Greek, *Hagia Sophia*).

It is one of the most remarkable buildings ever erected anywhere. The finest materials known went into its construction: special light bricks from Rhodes for the enormous cupola, red porphyry columns from Rome, silver and gold work from Ephesus, verd antique from Thessaly, white marble from the islands of Marmara and yellow marble from Africa. Four acres of the interior were covered by glowing mosaics, in which gold predominated. The whole was like a vast jewel, lit by silver candelabra.

The dome was soon damaged by earthquake, and reinforcement has coarsened the outward appearance. Supporting buttresses were put in place in the 14th century. The minarets were added after the Turkish Conquest of 1453, when St. Sophia was converted into a mosque. Sinan strengthened the buttresses in the 16th century, and the most recent restoration was carried

Soaring like the vault of heaven, St. Sophia's enormous dome is highlighted by calligraphy in gold.

out in the middle years of the last century. In 1935 Atatürk proclaimed St. Sophia a museum.

Visitors enter by a side door, passing through the vestibule to the inner narthex. This opens through nine doorways into the nave, a space of dramatically lofty proportions topped by the stupendous **cupola,** approximately 31 metres (100 ft.) in diameter and 55 metres (180 ft.) high. Earthquakes and restoration have squeezed it into a less than perfect circle. Arabic calligraphy around the apex of the dome was placed there after restoration in 1847, complementing panels inscribed in Arabic with Islamic holy names.

St. Sophia was a church for about 1,000 years, a mosque for 500. The Crusaders were responsible for plundering its treasures and divesting it of its glory. Mehmet the Conqueror's first act on taking Constantinople was to visit St. Sophia, and the first ritual prayers of the new ruler were performed here.

The apse contains one of the finest **mosaics:** the Virgin Mary holding the infant Jesus, with a striking figure of the Archangel Gabriel on the supporting arch. His companion archangel, Michael, has vanished, but for a few feathers from his wings. Mount the sloping corridors leading from the narthex to the galleries for other examples. Opposite the Deesis, an extraordinary 13th-century mosaic showing Jesus flanked by the Virgin and St. John the Baptist, is the empty tomb of Enrico Dandolo, Doge of Venice, the man most responsible for the mindless pillaging of Constantinople in 1204. Several other mosaics show emperors and empresses presenting gifts to the Holy Mother and Child.

Before leaving, pay a visit to the **Weeping Column** with a thumb-sized hole which remains perpetually damp because of water absorption from subterranean level. Christian legend says it's the impression of St. Gregory's finger; Muslims claim it's the spot where a holy man inserted his finger to try to turn the building towards Mecca.

Underground Palace

What about a change of focus with a visit to a cistern? Not just any cistern. This is fascinating **Yerebatan Sarayı** (Sunken Palace), a stone's throw from the Hippodrome. You descend to a vast, man-made cavern, given its name in the 6th century when Justinian enlarged the original cistern built by Constantine the Great. Yerebatan Sarayı is the most famous of many water storage tanks in Istanbul. Water from the Belgrade Forest, north of Istanbul, was held here for use if the city were besieged. The

336 Byzantine columns with Corinthian capitals and the brick arches are still securely in place, reflected in dark water which stretches out of sight in a hushed twilight, 14 centuries old.

Topkapı Palace

Ancient residence of the Ottoman sultans, *Topkapı Sarayı* was built by Mehmet the Conqueror in 1462. Every succeeding sultan added something to the palace, which gradually became a royal city comprising mosques, bathhouses, mint, schools, libraries, residences, gardens and fountains, built around four main courtyards.

Near to the outer entrance to Topkapı is a particularly graceful **fountain** erected in the early 18th century by Ahmet III. Exquisite fountains proliferate in Turkey, where a gift of clear water to the populace is a traditional charitable gesture.

The First Court is entered through the Imperial Gate *(Bab-ı Hümayun)*, built in 1478. Then come gardens, lawns and sweeping trees, providing the right dreamlike atmosphere for penetrating further into the mysterious universe of the sultans. This area is known as the **Court of the Janissaries** after the military corps which once assembled here. Nothing remains of the former palace services such as bakeries and buildings for storing firewood; nevertheless the First Court has a treasure: the old church of St. Irene. Postpone your visit for now and continue to the fortified Gate of Salutations *(Bab-üs Selam)*. The building where the ticket office is housed occasionally served as a prison; the executioner cleaned up and rinsed his sword in the nearby fountain after a beheading. No one but the sultan could pass through the gate on horseback, and it is still the point where all cars and taxis have to stop. It leads to the Court of the Divan, where the imperial council met, the beginning of the palace proper.

Stylized flowers bloom in profusion on every wall of Topkapı palace.

To the right of the gate lie the enormous **kitchens** built by Mehmet the Conqueror and Beyazıt II in the 15th century, considerably enlarged since then. Apart from cooking areas, there were mosques, baths and dormitories for the various chefs, pastry-makers and scullions.

Today the kitchens house a priceless collection of **Chinese porcelain** as well as European crystal and porcelain, Ottoman cooking implements and serving dishes. There are 10,512 pieces of Chinese porcelain alone at Topkapı, of which the majority has to be kept in storage.

But this is only a start to the palace treasures. If nothing else, you must visit the **harem**. In origin the word means "sacred" or "set apart". The sultan, his mother, wives (of whom he was allowed four) and innumerable concubines all lived in this dim network of staircases, corridors, bedrooms and bathrooms, in a stifling world of ambitious intrigue. The main preoccupation of the womenfolk was to produce a male child, and then to assure his accession to the throne. It was a claustrophobic, unnatural world of jealousy and unhappiness; you may sense the troubled atmosphere lingering in the dusty sunlight and complicated decor.

Apart from the sultan, the only adult males allowed in the harem were the black eunuchs who guarded it. You pass through the carriage gate, the exit used by the women on their rare outings, to the **black eunuchs' dormitory**. The sticks on the wall were used to beat the guilty—and the innocent—on the soles of the feet, a mandatory punishment regularly applied to all novices.

The sultan's mother, or *valide sultan*, held unique power over her son, the empire and especially the harem. Her **apartments** occupy most of the building west of the Courtyard of the Valide Sultan. The bed-place with its gilded canopy is faced with 17th-century flowered tiles. The small prayer-room alongside shows scenes from Mecca and Medina.

The **Baths of the Sultan** comprise a dressing room, a cool room and the baths themselves. The sultan was bathed by elderly female servants, then attended by groups of younger handmaids wearing stilted clogs of the type still seen in Turkish antique shops, although here they were most often sheathed with beaten silver.

Pass into the luxuriant **Hall of the Sultan**, with three handsome marble fountains and the canopied throne from which the sultan would watch dancing,

Peaceloving aesthete, Sultan Selim III was brutally stabbed to death.

listen to music or enjoy plays or puppet shows. The mother sultana and official wives sat on the raised platform while the more musically talented slave-girls performed from the balcony.

The suite of rooms known as the **Pavilion of Murat III** is the most amazing of all, boasting inlaid floors, flowered Iznik tiles of the best period, carved fountains and fireplaces, with a superb dome in the main chamber attributed to Sinan; the ensemble forming the epitome of 16th-century Turkish design. Don't miss the small Library (early 17th century), and the Fruit Room (early 18th century) painted in European rococo style with flowers and fruit for Ahmet III, the "Tulip King", who greeted spring every year with a tulip festival in the palace grounds.

Gold glistens in abundance in the **Treasury**, where the display starts modestly enough with a bowl of apple-green peridots, then explodes into wild magnificence: you can gaze at a pair of solid gold candlesticks, each encrusted with 666 diamonds (representing the 666 verses of the Koran); a golden throne studded with over 900 peridots; a silver-gilt cradle decorated with pearls, in which new-born princes and princesses were presented to the sultan; another throne, gold plate over wood, ornamented with enamel and precious stones.

Stars of the collection are an 86-carat diamond surrounded by 49 smaller stones, known as the Spoonmaker's Diamond, displayed in the fourth hall of the Treasury and, of course, presented with suitable bravura in the second hall, the dagger rendered famous by the film, *Topkapi*. The handle contains three huge emeralds winking green fire, with a fourth on top serving as cover to a watch embedded in the hilt. The gold sheath is set with diamonds.

St. Irene

Back in Topkapı's First Court, the **Church of St. Irene** *(Aya İrini Kilisesi)* awaits a visit. It was built by Justinian in the form of a domed basilica, more or less at the same time as St. Sophia. The name means "divine peace", which did nothing to dissuade the Janissaries from using it as an arms depot. Recently the church has undergone restoration, and concerts are held here, especially during the Istanbul Festival in June.

Museums

Three exceptional museums are placed conveniently next to one another in a nearby courtyard. Even if you're not a history-lover, don't miss the **Archaeological Museum** *(Arkeoloji Müzesi)*, especially reputed for its collection of sarcophagi.

The **Museum of the Ancient Orient** *(Eski Şark Eserleri Müzesi)* displays a rich collection of objects from ancient Near and Middle Eastern civilizations. Among them figure Babylonian panels from the time of King Nebuchadnezzar (605–562 B.C.), enigmatically smiling statuettes from Mesopotamia and clay tablets bearing Hammurabi's law code in cuneiform lettering.

The most eye-catching building in this square, the **Tiled Pavilion** *(Çinili Köşkü)*, built by Mehmet the Conqueror in 1472, was designed as a hunting lodge and has remained practically unchanged. The exterior tiles are mostly from the Seljuk period. Inside is a valuable display of ceramics from Seljuk times to the 20th century.

Central District

A broad, straight road, Divan Yolu, runs all the way from Sultan Ahmet Square to Beyazıt Square, the most animated area of the old city, set on the Third Hill. It was a main street in Byzantine times, just as it is today. On the right, almost midway along, rises the **Burnt Column**, or *Çemberlitaş,* charred by a great fire which raged here in 1770. Constantine erected it in May 330 to mark the city's new status as capital of the Roman Empire. As well as pagan relics,

nails from the Cross on which Christ was crucified and part of the Cross itself were reputed to be sealed in the base.

Behind the Burnt Column, the Baroque exterior of **Nuruosmaniye Camii** (1755) contrasts with the simplicity of the interior, where 174 windows reflect the meaning of the name of the mosque: "Light of Osman".

Beyazıt Square and Mosque

Pigeons wheel over the crowds in **Beyazıt Meydanı** as they have throughout the 1,600 years of its existence. Theodosius I had the square laid out in the 4th century, adding a triumphal arch in his own name as a nice finishing touch. Hefty fragments can be seen off the south-west corner.

The noble **mosque** which dominates the north-east side was built by Sultan Beyazıt, son of Mehmet the Conqueror, in the very early years of the 16th century. This peace-loving mystic, in every way the antithesis of his energetic father, thereby became responsible for the beginning of classical Ottoman architecture, drawing inspiration directly from St. Sophia. The buildings which once formed part of the mosque complex—schools, inn and public baths—are now mostly converted to other uses.

Take a moment's breather

under the ancient dappled plane tree in the tea garden between the mosque and the university to observe Istanbul's student life, before you enter the Grand Bazaar. The **Beyazıt Tower,** looming in the university grounds beyond the big monumental gates, was a fire lookout, placed there in 1828. Athletic visitors can climb 179 steps for a memorable panoramic view.

Grand Bazaar

Covered market, *Kapalı Çarşı*—call it what you will, the Grand Bazaar looks like Ali Baba's cave and sounds like the trading post for the Tower of Babel. This is

Market gossip—the same gestures the world over.

the biggest oriental market in the world. It's like a complete city, with a many-domed roof. There are quiet alleys, lively crossroads and main streets.

Mehmet the Conqueror had a covered market built on the site in 1461. It has been reconstructed several times after destruction by fire and earthquake. Nowadays it contains about 4,000 shops, as well as banks, cafés, restaurants and mosques. The most ancient part is the Old Bedesten at the centre, kept for more valuable merchandise since it can be securely locked at night.

Even if you've no intention of buying anything, visit the Covered Market for a distillation of Istanbul and Turkey. It's a kaleidoscope of constantly changing brilliance. Voices call out in a dozen languages. Watersellers come jangling by; incredibly strong men, *hamal,* lumber past, harnessed into a kind of leather saddle and transporting anything up to a sofa and chairs on their backs.

Afterwards, the **Book Market** (*Sahaflar Çarşısı*) comes as a much-needed respite. There are works in every language. You're quite likely to find a gorgeously illuminated Koran not far from a copy of Plato's *Republic*, or a faded photograph of Sinatra propped up on a well-thumbed copy of Donald Duck.

Mosque of Suleiman the Magnificent

Sober in outline, harmonious in its classic proportions, the *Süleymaniye* is beautifully positioned above the Golden Horn, a tribute to two men of genius, Suleiman, the sultan who saw the Ottoman Empire to the zenith of its power, and Sinan, his chief architect. The mosque was built between 1550 and 1557 by some 5,300 workmen.

You enter through a broad courtyard with a rectangular marble and gilt bronze ablutions fountain. Daylight floods into the interior through 16th-century stained glass windows. The **dome** is 53 metres (175 ft.) high, the interior of the mosque itself measures 57 by 60 metres (187 by 197 ft.). Four porphyry columns mark its corners. Iznik tiles are set either side of the *mihrab.* Doors and shutters are fastidiously worked with ivory and mother-of-pearl.

According to legend, jewels from Persia were mixed with the cement for the buildings, and the incredible acoustics were attained by embedding 64 hollow jars neck-down in the dome. Try making the slightest sound at the base of one of the pillars and you'll hear it amplified and repeated in echoes. It's said, too, that Suleiman recognized greatness when he saw it: he gave the keys of the mosque to Sinan, and it was the architect, not the sultan, who opened it.

Suleiman the Magnificent, also called "the Great" and "the Lawgiver", reigned for 46 years from his accession in 1520. During this golden age, the arts and sciences flourished. The Süleymaniye is considered the finest of all the mosques in Istanbul for the harmony of its domes, cupolas and arcades.

Both the sultan and the architect (who was almost 100 when he died) are buried in the grounds. Take time for a stroll there. When in season, irises, roses and mauve hollyhocks tangle in long grass between leaning gravestones, while sparrows swoop and squabble in the fig trees. Sinan lies in a modest mausoleum on the periphery of the grounds, while Suleiman has a far grander tomb, decorated with Iznik tiles and original painting, the imperial turban at his head. The tomb of Suleiman's wife Roxelana is also decorated with magnificent Iznik tiles.

Walking around the terrace, which affords a superb view towards Galata Bridge, you'll be aware of the immensity of the whole complex, which included bath-houses, schools, caravanserai, a library, kitchens, a refuge for the poor and houses for attendants. You'll also be able to note the minarets: two with two balconies, the other two with three. Four minarets signify that Suleiman was the fourth sultan to reign in Istanbul; the total of ten balconies indicates that he was the tenth monarch to lead the Ottoman Empire.

Outer City

There's a whole garland of mosques and Byzantine churches looping through this neighbourhood, which becomes more picturesque as you work your way towards St. Saviour in Chora and down to the Balat and Fener districts along the Golden Horn. Anatolian families moving to Istanbul add colour to old districts, where you have to pick your way over cobbles and the occasional unpaved rocky track between tottering wooden houses strung with washing. You may even be a bit of a curiosity yourself, but the interest will be friendly.

Start at Şehzadebaşı Caddesi. The imposing **Mosque of the Prince** *(Şehzade Camii)* is one of Sinan's early works, completed in 1548. It was constructed as a memorial for Suleiman the Magnificent's son, Prince Mehmet, who died in 1543 at the age of 21.

From there, strutting in fine style across Atatürk Bulvarı, are the remains of the **Valens Aqueduct** *(Bozdoğan Kemeri)*, whose pedigree goes back to the 2nd century. The Emperor Valens had it rebuilt in the 4th century; it has been restored several times since, and was still in use during the last century. In its heyday the aqueduct supplied water to a central cistern, first for the Byzantine palace, later for Topkapı. You can sit below the arches in the garden courtyard of a serene, 16th-century building, now the **Municipal Museum** *(Belediye Müzesi)*, which is worth a visit for paintings of old Istanbul and a dusty but endearing clutter of photographs, costumes, glassware, writing effects and assorted memorabilia.

Mehmet the Conqueror and his family are buried in the grounds of **Fatih Camii**, built on the Fourth Hill between 1462 and 1470, but reconstructed after an earthquake in 1766. The extensive complex, biggest in the whole Ottoman Empire, included a hospital, a mental asylum, poorhouses, and accommodation for visitors, irrespective of race and religion. Numerous schools taught science, mathematics and history as well as religious law. At the time, such enlightened philanthropy and education were unusual anywhere in the world.

Take Yavuz Selim Caddesi for a view of fig trees, apple trees, neat vegetable patches and the red-tiled roofs of little houses, all planted below the road and surrounded by the remains of Roman walls, in front of the Mosque of Selim I. This pretty village occupies the dried-out Cistern of Aspar, and is known in Turkish as **Çukurbostan** (Sunken Garden).

Dominating the Fifth Hill, the **Mosque of Selim I** *(Sultan Selim Camii)* is dedicated to Suleiman the Magnificent's father. Pass through the colourful courtyard to look out over the sluggish waters of the Golden Horn, and you'll catch sight of St. George's, the Greek Orthodox Patriarchate. Below is the district of Fener and further up the Golden Horn is Balat. To wander through these narrow streets is to witness another Istanbul. Sit on a doorstep (no one will mind) and watch the children playing old and strangely familiar street games, while their mothers, clad in vivid trousers and modest headscarves, and their grandmothers, swathed in black, chat in groups, pausing for a glance or a shy smile in your direction.

Chickens squawk in the courtyard of the **Church of Theotokos Pammakaristos** *(Fethiye Camii)*, and washing flaps among piles of masonry. One part of the building is retained for Christian worship, the other is a mosque. Examine what remains of the series of 14th-century mosaics which once adorned the church.

51

One of the brightest jewels in Istanbul's Byzantine crown is the former church of St. Saviour in Chora, **Kariye Camii**, now a museum containing outstanding frescoes and mosaics. When the church was built it stood outside the city walls, justifying the Greek name *Chora*, meaning "countryside".

The oldest part is the central domed area, dated 1120. The church was rebuilt early in the 14th century by Theodore Metochites, statesman, scholar and art-lover, close friend and advisor to the Emperor Andronicus II Palaeologus. Sadly, this cultured humanist was reduced to poverty when the emperor was overthrown and saw out the last years of his life in Chora monastery among the glorious works of art with which he had embellished it. He outlived Andronicus by only one month.

Metochites left the central structure untouched but probably added the outer narthex and the parecclesion or side-chapel. The church was converted into a mosque in 1511 but was not altered, apart from the addition of a minaret and the sealing up of some windows. Wooden screens were placed over the **mosaics**. These are usually grouped into six categories and depict the life of Jesus and the Virgin Mary. The mosaic over the door leading into the nave has a likeness of Metochites presenting his beloved church to Christ. To intensify the effect of light, each tile was set at a slightly different depth and angle, creating a shimmering, moving surface.

Meticulous restoration of old wooden dwellings complements the mellow brickwork of St. Saviour in Chora.

52

All the **frescoes** are in the parecclesion, which stretches the whole length of the building and was used in Byzantine times as a funerary chapel. There, in the semi-dome of the apse, is the masterly Resurrection *(Anastasis)*.

The mosaics and frescoes may be by the same artist and are contemporaneous with Giotto's work in Padua, dating from 1310–1320. They are sometimes attributed to the Greek, Theophanes. Subtlety of colour, liveliness of posture and the strong, lifelike faces of the subjects all attest to a last extraordinary flowering of Byzantine art before its descent into decadence.

Marking the Sixth Hill is **Mihrimah Camii**, built by Sinan in 1565 for one of Suleiman's daughters. Further north lies an

old palace, **Tekfur Sarayı**, part of the last major residence of the Byzantine imperial family.

Mehmet the Conqueror entered the city through the **Adrianople Gate** *(Edirnekapı)* in the nearby **Theodosian Walls**, which were originally constructed in the 5th century. At their grandest they stretched for 17 kilometres (12 mi.) from the Sea of Marmara to the Golden Horn, were fortified by 400 towers and had 50 gates of which 7 remain in use. Much of the inner wall and many of the towers are still standing.

Camping among the rubble of the proud old ramparts are Istanbul's gypsies. They have been there off and on since the 12th century when emperor Andronicus Comnenus gave them the right to set up a shanty-town, known today as Sulukule.

At the Marmara end of the Theodosian Walls, a long way from the other sights of Istanbul but easily reached by the coast road, stands the ancient fortress known as **Seven Towers** *(Yedikule)*. The four Byzantine and three Turkish towers were enclosed within walls by Mehmet the Conqueror in 1470. The nearby **Golden Gate** *(Altınkapı)* existed before the construction of the city walls and was heavily decorated with marble reliefs and gold inscriptions. It was the magnificent triumphal arch of the Byzantine emperors.

Eminönü

Leave yourself the time for a leisurely walk through the district of Eminönü, where Galata Bridge meets the the Golden Horn. Here the crowds seem at their most frenetic, the babble of voices the loudest, the odours and colours the strongest, for Eminönü is the synopsis of all the sights, sounds and smells of old Istanbul.

The square before the **New Mosque** *(Yeni Cami* or *Valide Camii),* is a congregating spot for some of Istanbul's better established beggars and pedlars who have set themselves up semi-permanently in front of the 17th-century building. Seated among them, dozing in the sun, are the grain-sellers from whom, for a few liras, you can buy a cupful of seed to minister to the pigeon population.

Begun by Mehmet III's mother in 1597, the New Mosque was completed 66 years later by the mother of Mehmet IV. It contains spectacular tiles, especially in the royal gallery, reached by a separate staircase.

The Egyptian or **Spice Market** *(Mısır Çarşısı)* just alongside was set up to raise money for repairs to the mosque complex. The air is heady with the scent of ginger, pepper, saffron, eucalyptus, jasmine, incense, cinnamon, nutmeg, rosewater and freshly roasted coffee beans. In the past, the sellers used to sit cross-legged on carpets, ready to seize pestle and mortar for pounding potions both efficacious and fanciful, optimistically prepared to cure anything from lumbago to love-sickness, from simple cases of sore throats to highly complicated cases of combating the Evil Eye. Nor were they all charlatans. Some of the market's herbal remedies are still available, even though they no longer contain such rare ingredients as ambergris, dragon's blood and tortoise eggs.

More mundane merchandise is available, too, for the Spice Market is a popular shopping complex for anything anyone could

Sugar and spice
and all things nice in the exotic
market of Eminönü.

55

need. Fish, flowers, clothing, secondhand shoes, wire netting, an astonishing selection of plastic buckets: all these and more are sold in the nearby streets.

Take time out in the **Mosque of Rüstem Pasha** (*Rüstempaşa Camii*) whose minaret soars over Hasırcılar Caddesi. Another of Sinan's masterpieces, it glows inside and out with fine Iznik tiles.

Work your way along Hamidiye Caddesi to **Sirkeci Railway Station**, erstwhile terminus for the famous Orient Express. Then, to catch the full flavour of the district, join the crowds and walk **Galata Bridge**, pausing first to descend underneath and explore the dozens of little fish restaurants and coffee shops, where Turkish men puff euphorically at their water pipes, staring out over the indefatigable water-traffic of the Golden Horn.

The first bridge at this point was built in 1845 by Abdul Mecit's mother. The existing structure, built in 1912 with German know-how, floats on pontoons; the central section is opened every morning for an hour to allow tall ships to pass through.

As you cross towards the northern bank you'll see, straight ahead, rising from the district that used to be called Galata and is now Karaköy, the unmistakable outline of the Galata Tower.

MODERN ISTANBUL

Names may change and districts lose their character, but **Galata** still clings to the remnants of its rip-roaring reputation, and will do so as long as there's a handful of true Galatiotes left to remember it.

Some time during the 11th century, a rough bunch of cast-off seamen and dubious drifters from every port in Europe and Asia settled along the edge of the Horn in the maritime quarter which became known as Galata. Genoese merchants had already taken up residence in the hills above the port, gradually establishing a fortified city within a city, calling themselves the Magnificent Community of Pera.

The **Galata Tower**, erected to defend this autonomous colony, is of uncertain date. It seems to have been built in 1349 in its present form, as a stronghold in the city walls. Architecturally of limited interest, the view from the restaurant at the top is fantastic. See it in the late evening when sky, water and buildings are stained lavender and rose by the sunset, and Istanbul takes on its most photogenic aspect

Out of the sea and into the frying pan—below Galata Bridge.

of nostalgic mystery. West and south you look out over the Horn; east lies the Bosphorus and the Tophane district, marked by Sinan's Kılıç Ali Paşa Camii and a 19th-century westernized structure, Nusretiye Camii. Between the two stands a light-hearted rococo confection often depicted in old drawings of Istanbul—the Tophane Fountain.

One of the oldest subways in the world, the *Tünel*, starts below the tower near the Galata Bridge and rumbles a short distance to the beginning of **İstiklâl Caddesi**, the main street of Beyoğlu. Palatial embassies were built along the road from the late 17th century onwards; trees fanned graceful gardens and a brilliant cosmopolitan crowd promenaded the most fashionable avenue in town.

The embassies remain, reduced to consulates since the transfer of the capital to Ankara in 1923. At Galatasaray Square where İstiklâl Caddesi changes direction, a supremely elegant gateway announces Galatasaray Lisesi, the Franco-Turkish *lycée* which was founded in the 19th century and provided education for many of the great names in modern Turkish history.

Maybe change pace by sidetracking down **Çiçek Pasajı** (Passage of Flowers), a narrow lane to the left past the Galatasaray intersection, favourite haunt of the town's rowdy Bohemia. Best (and worst!) at night, it's crowded with a rag-tail, raucous bunch of gypsies, fortune-tellers, down-at-heel poets and visitors, all meeting, drinking and swapping yarns in innumerable taverns. A word to the wise: plant your valuables in a safe place before you go.

A different experience awaits visitors to the **Pera Palas Hotel** on Meşrutiyet Caddesi, established in 1892 for Orient Express passengers. Its splendour is faded now, but that only adds to the charm of the vast, chandeliered public areas with antique braziers and samovars and thick Turkish carpets. The cage-elevator will carry you up to view Atatürk's room, kept as it was when he stayed here.

Today's İstiklâl Caddesi is a busy commercial thoroughfare lined with boutiques, roaring with traffic. Yet, just here and there, you'll come across a high-ceilinged ice-cream parlour, a dignified pastry shop, redolent of the past.

The street ends at **Taksim Meydanı**, heart of the modern city, site of the big, new Atatürk Cultural Centre. In the summer, during the International Festival, concert tickets are sold here, and numerous performances staged.

Above Taksim is the "hotel district", and beyond again is the

Military Museum *(Askeri Müze)*, opposite the Sports and Exhibition Hall at Harbiye. Don't be put off by its name: it's a fascinating place, and your visit will be all the more rewarding if you turn up in time for a concert by the Mehter Band, a revival of the Janissaries' music ensemble. Their brief, rousing displays are enjoyed by everyone, not least of all by the musicians themselves. (Performances are held every day at 3 p.m. except Monday and Tuesday when the museum is closed.)

Dolmabahçe

A broad road running downhill from Harbiye joins Dolmabahçe Caddesi, the tree-lined boulevard edging along the Bosphorus past **Dolmabahçe Palace.**

Pass through the ornately decorated gateway. There, dreaming among pines and magnolias, frosty white against the blue of the Bosphorus, is a 19th-century fantasy of scrolled and colonnaded marble, almost naive in its romanticism. In its way Dolmabahçe is symbolic. Built between 1843 and 1856 for Sultan Abdul Mecit, it was the residence of the last sultans. This dazzling exterior and a glittering interior provided the intimate setting for the final hours of the Ottoman Empire. Forced to admit the strength of Turkey's claims for democracy, the last sultan left Dolmabahçe in a British warship.

When Atatürk opened the palace to the public he proclaimed that the "Shadows of God" (the sultans) had been replaced by "real people, who are not shadows" and ended, "I am here as the guest of the nation." The burst of applause was enough to set Dolmabahçe's chandeliers chiming like crystal bells.

For this is a crystal palace: there are 36 chandeliers hung throughout, complemented by numerous Baccarat and Bohemian fixtures, light fittings and mirrors; even the staircase leading from the entry hall has a crystal handrail. Damask-covered chairs, alabaster bathroom, Sèvres vases, enamel-work, Gobelin and Turkish silk carpets, porphyry, porcelain, silver, two huge bearskins (gifts from the Tsar of Russia)—just to enumerate a few of the contents emphasizes the unreality of the last days of the empire.

Through this outdated world the spirit of Atatürk swept like a breeze. Early work on the westernization of the Turkish alphabet was carried out here. Atatürk maintained a small apartment for himself and died at Dolmabahçe on November 10, 1938. Palace clocks have been stopped at 9.05, the time of his death.

The **Maritime Museum** *(Deniz Müzesi)* and the **Painting and Sculpture Museum** *(Resim ve Heykel Müzesi)* are both in this area. Visit the latter for its landscapes showing Istanbul as a city of gardens and wooded hills, and to trace 19th- and 20th-century evolution of Turkish art.

Wooded hills are for real in **Yıldız Park**, as well as lakes, rivulets and winding paths. Two kiosks and a pavilion have been restored by Çelik Gülersoy, the man responsible for preserving many buildings from Istanbul's past. The palace here, **Yıldız Sarayı**, was a royal residence for 30 years in the time of Sultan Abdul Hamid II (1876–1909), who preferred it to Dolmabahçe.

Further up where the Bosphorus is narrowest broods **Rumeli Hisarı**, a fortress built by Mehmet II in 1452 in preparation for the Conquest and restored in 1953. Consisting of three major citadels linked by stone walls, it is a stupendous feat of construction, accomplished in only four months. Nowadays the interior contains a park and a theatre where folk-dancing and plays are performed.

The two faces of Istanbul: "Western" sophistication at Dolmabahçe; Anatolian folklore.

ASIAN SHORE

Ferries leave regularly from the Galata Bridge for Üsküdar and other points on the Asian shore. By car or coach you'll cross the Bosphorus higher up over the impressive **Bosphorus Bridge**, with a main span of 1,074 metres (3,524 ft.). It was completed in 1973 and opened for the 50th anniversary of the founding of the Turkish Republic.

At the Asian exit is **Beylerbeyi Palace**, less magnificent than Dolmabahçe but still a marvel of opulent furnishing and shimmering crystal, surrounded by gardens. It was reconstructed in 1865 on the site of an earlier palace, destroyed by fire.

The road which follows the Bosphorus northward leads to **Anadolu Hisarı**, a fortress facing Rumeli Hisarı on the opposite bank, but pre-dating it by about 60 years, built by the Turks as a preliminary to seizing Constantinople.

Directly inland from the Bosphorus Bridge, the park and lookout point of **Çamlıca** offers a bucolic refuge for viewing Istanbul. The extensive cypress-studded cemetery you see is **Karacaahmet**, one of the largest Islamic burial grounds in the world. South lies **Üsküdar**, better known to Europeans as Scutari, from where the ferries ply to the European shore. There, among many religious buildings,

note **Iskele Camii** (1548), another mosque designed by Sinan for Suleiman's daughter, Mihrimah, and the **New Mosque of the Mother Sultana** *(Yeni Valide Camii),* dating from the early 18th century.

Scutari is associated with the name of Florence Nightingale. In bulky **Selimiye Kışlası,** the barracks sternly surveying the straits, the Lady with the Lamp set up her hospital for soldiers wounded in the Crimean War. Nearby is the well-kept Crimean War Cemetery.

EXCURSIONS

No matter how many monuments you've visited or how much atmosphere you've absorbed, you still don't really know Istanbul until you've seen it from the water. All the main ferries leave from alongside the Eminönü end of the Galata Bridge.

Bosphorus

You'll weave from Europe to Asia and back again along the historic waterway, idling below pine-clad hills until you're within sight of the Black Sea. Some of the buildings will be familiar but from here they have a fresh aspect, and you'll realize how carefully architects of long ago planned them with exactly this intention.

Outstanding among landmarks is **Kılıç Ali Paşa Camii** at Tophane, followed by the monumental 19th-century cannon factory. Then, looking like a stone ship about to push off into the water, comes the **Molla Çelebi Camii,** erected in the middle years of the 16th century. **Dolmabahçe Palace** sails into sight, then the skeletal walls of **Çırağan Palace,** destroyed by fire in 1910.

You'll chug under the leaping

arch of the **Bosphorus Bridge**, to see **Beylerbeyi Palace** in Asia, the two vastly differing structures providing an illuminating juxtaposition of the introverted final years of the Ottoman Empire and the forward-looking aims of the Turkish Republic.

Next comes the most picturesque section, which may well tempt you to stop off for some leisurely exploring. On the Asian shore at Küçüksu and Anadolu

Rumeli Hisarı, a pleasant enclave overlooking the Bosphorus, was built to defend Constantinople.

Hisarı, calm streams, which Europeans called the Sweet Waters of Asia, emerge under dusky foliage. Mirrored beyond are some of the few remaining *yalı*, wooden houses built at the very lip of the water, dilapidated now, their painted weatherboards worn bare by the elements. Such summer dwellings, with a boathouse underneath, were designed for the enjoyment of two things most dear to the Turks: the sight of trees and flowers and the soft music of the water. Almost impossibly costly to maintain nowadays, dozens have been demolished. This little group is one of the finest.

Rumeli Hisarı on the European side and **Anadolu Hisarı** opposite crouch in centuries-old defiance where the straits narrow. Then comes the **Tarabya** district with its famous fish and seafood restaurants and cosmopolitan atmosphere. From Beykoz, the next stop in Asia, you can take a taxi to the Black Sea resort of **Şile** for excellent bathing beaches; Sarıyer in Europe is where you drop off for an equivalent excursion to **Kilyos**. Finally, there's Rumeli Kavağı (Europe) and Anadolu Kavağı (Asia), both sleepy villages whose fish restaurants make ideal luncheon spots.

The one-way trip takes two hours, but don't hesitate to break your journey: there's plenty of land transport available on the European side to return you to Istanbul.

Golden Horn

This is not a scenic trip in the normal sense but a view through the city's industrial back door at factories and shipbuilding yards all the way to **Eyüp**.

There, follow the crowds to the **mosque** *(Eyüp Sultan Camii),* supposed burial place of Eyüp Ensari, the Prophet Muhammad's standard-bearer. He came with an Arab army to besiege Constantinople and was killed by an arrow some time between 674 and 678. The grave was rediscovered as the result of a vision; Mehmet the Conqueror built a shrine on the spot. He then had a mosque erected in 1458, his first in Istanbul and one of the most sacred in the Muslim world. It was visited by each sultan on accession to the throne for the ceremony of girding on the dynastic sword. In 1800 Selim III rebuilt the mosque.

There are many tombs in the environs, but the crowds are most intent on paying homage to Eyüp himself, interred in a tiled sanctum protected by a golden grid.

Behind the mosque is a hillside **cemetery** with many old turbaned tombs; a path winds up to a café known as the "Pierre Loti café", in honour of the French writer who often climbed to this windy summit, during his visit in 1876, to muse over the distant minarets of Istanbul melting into the twilight. One of Loti's relatives donated photographs from the period, now on display in an intimate museum.

Princes Islands

When you need a rest from strenuous sightseeing, escape to this delightful retreat in the Sea of Marmara. Of the nine islands, **Büyükada** (Principio) is the largest and most visited. Runners-up are **Kınalı**, **Burgaz** and **Heybeli**. There are no museums, no cars even, just horses and carriages to get around (the alternative is riding a donkey), grand houses wreathed with wisteria and bougainvillea, pine forests, cliffs and swimming places.

You'll need a complete day for a leisurely visit, but avoid weekends, when the whole of Istanbul has the same idea.

Bursa

The boat which goes to Princes Islands usually continues to the little port and spa town of Yalova, from where land transport is available to Bursa. Coach tours and flights from Istanbul are available, too. The distance is far enough to necessitate an overnight stay.

The fringe of the Sea of Marmara is largely industrial. It has a ghostly look, especially in the early morning. Land, water and sky seem to merge, while steamers and rowboats pass like shadows, trailing dark lines in the colourless water as they cross towards Yalova.

Inland, the countryside takes on the gentle contours typical of this region, known in ancient times as Bithynia. Poplars and walnut trees flourish in the valleys, olive groves clothe the slopes; south of Gemlik the peach orchards begin. Then there's a wide plain with Ulu Dağ, the Great Mountain, dominating the horizon, protective backdrop to Bursa.

This friendly, airy little city, founded in the 2nd century B.C. by King Prusias I, was known as Prusa after him. It became the Ottoman capital in the 14th century, then Edirne took over as seat of government.

Outstanding among monuments is the **Tomb of Osman Gazi** *(Osman Gazi Türbesi)*, founder of the Line of Osman and hence of the Ottoman Empire. He died in 1324 in the neighbouring town of Söğüt, but was buried in Bursa at his own request in what was formerly a Byzantine chapel. Lead plates in the dome once shone like silver. Complemented by the silver-embroidered drape on the sarcophagus, they caused his resting-place to be known as the "silver tomb". **Orhan Türbesi**, the tomb of Osman's son who lies nearby, was built on the site of a monastery. Fragments of its ancient mosaic pavement can be seen on the floor of the tomb.

The admirable **Green Mosque** *(Yeşil Cami)* takes its name from the dizzying beauty of its tiled interior. Both it and the **Green Tomb** *(Yeşil Türbe)* opposite were built by the same architect, Hacı İvaz Paşa, for the 15th-century sultan, Mehmet I.

Stone from Bursa's own Great Mountain was quarried for the **Great Mosque** *(Ulu Cami)*, constructed in the last years of the 14th century. Twenty domes crown its rectangular area; the central one, over the ablutions fountain, was originally left open, then glassed in later.

Take time, too, for the **Muradiye mosque complex,** built in the 1420s for Murat II, father of Mehmet the Conqueror, and the last sultan to rule from Bursa.

The town boasts a number of old-style houses with overhanging balconies shaded by vines. Call in at the 18th-century two-storey building, opposite the Muradiye, to see how wealthier private dwellings were furnished.

Bursa's other attractions include a newly reconstructed covered market, part of which extends into the **Koza Hanı**, first built in 1451. Nowadays this arcaded caravanserai is the centre of the silk cocoon market: look down from the rooms into the courtyard to see the cocoons being sorted and sold.

The most remarkable of all the thermal baths in the area is an Art-Deco marvel in the **Çelik Palas Hotel**. Right alongside, a 19th-century building garnished with wood-carving in typical Victorian colonial style houses the **Atatürk Museum**.

Two other museums merit a visit. Pigeons fly through the arched doorways of the **Museum of Turkish and Islamic Art** *(Türk ve İslam Eserleri Müzesi)* in the Green Mosque's *medrese*, one of the religious buildings which formed part of the mosque complex. The **Archaeological Museum** *(Arkeoloji Müzesi)* in the Culture Park houses a number of Archaic, Hellenistic, Roman and Byzantine finds. (Both museums are closed Mondays.)

In the park, too, you may catch a display of Karagöz puppets. Although this type of shadow play probably originated in China, the characters which gained fame and affection in Turkey are based on two Bursa workmen, Karagöz and Hacivat. These were fellow labourers whose squabbles, jokes and tricks incurred the royal wrath of Sultan Orhan. They were put to death on his orders, but their earthy humour lives on, especially in Bursa where there is a modest monument commemorating them.

The Green Tomb in Bursa, once capital of the Ottoman Empire.

Troy *(Truva)*

Because of its situation on the far north of the Aegean coastline, Troy can be reached equally well from Izmir, Bursa or Istanbul. Çanakkale is the main centre for the region. From there local travel agencies arrange tours to the sites.

Seaside hotels south of Çanakkale, at Güzelyalı, provide an ideal spot for staying the night on the way to the ruins of the fabulous city which was, almost without doubt, Homer's Troy.

A small park at **Hisarlık** marks the entrance, and you can't miss the big wooden horse set up there. Beyond is everything—and nothing: those who come expecting grandeur will see just a limited area of excavations. For many, though, even with slight knowledge of the *Iliad* and the *Odyssey*, it's a magical place.

Here, according to legend most likely based on fact, lived peace-loving King Priam whose son, Paris, was inveigled by a trio of jealous goddesses into abducting the most beautiful woman in the world, Helen, wife of Menelaus, king of Sparta. The war which resulted between Greece and Troy lasted for ten long years. The end came when the Greeks tricked the Trojans into dragging a wooden horse filled with armed men within their walls. They sacked the city and left it a ruin.

In fact, there were nine Troys over the centuries, from a primitive Early Bronze Age settlement existing from 3000 to 2500 B.C. (Troy I), to the Hellenistic and Roman metropolis which stood here from 334 B.C. to A.D. 400, known as *Ilium Novum*. Oblivion may have begun when Istanbul took commercial precedence over this trade centre for the Dardanelles.

Troy's location remained in the realm of scholarly debate until a German amateur archaeologist with a passion for Homer—Heinrich Schliemann—began excavations in 1871. Disorderly as his work was, at a time when archaeology was in its infancy, it was Schliemann's faith, fortune and boundless energy which uncovered Troy.

American archaeologists tend to identify Troy VIIa as Priam's city and place its destruction at about 1260 B.C.; some eminent Turkish archaeologists disagree, attributing it to the level known as Troy VI. The second theory is certainly more appealing, for Troy VIIa was a mediocre, hastily constructed city, whereas its predecessor was a fine, solid town with a paved main street. It would be pleasant to think that the big southern gate was the Scaean Gate and that the large house supported internally by pillars was the palace of Priam. North-east are the remains of a well-built tower. Certainly, Troy VI fits more aptly with Homer's description of a "well-walled, well-towered, high-gated" city. It was razed by fire and earthquake. Yet Troy VIIa shows all the signs of a town under siege, with large subterranean food storage areas and confined accommodation for numbers of people. Moreover, it was destroyed by war and swept by fire.

For detailed information it's best to hire a guide, although the site is signposted. The most casual visitor will sense drama in the timeworn stones. The wind whistles through thickets of stunted oak and sets the wild flowers nodding.

Schliemann's house is maintained as a small museum, with photographs of him and his wife. His memory still evokes enthusiasm and criticism. And, yes, he did find "Priam's treasure", a great haul of jewellery alongside the city walls of Troy II. He cut it out with a knife, wrapped it in his wife's shawl and smuggled it away. It was last seen in Berlin but vanished during World War II.

On the coast, glorious beaches fringe the Gulf of Edremit, with Mount Ida (Kaz Dağı) to the east and, west, the lovely outline of the Greek island of Lesbos. Ayvalık is an ideal spot for enjoying it all. South again, Dikili is a picturesque fishing port.

THRACE

In eastern Thrace, all roads lead to Asia. This is Turkey's low country—for the most part a sleeping plain whose sunflowers wave you on through wide tracts of wheatfields to Istanbul, the natural exit of this funnel of land.

Most people pass through without a stop, some driving directly to Istanbul, others heading south via Gallipoli for the beaches of the Aegean. Either way Anatolia beckons, to the detriment of tiny Thrace. Once, it was different. Many a Thracian Turk will tell you to look back over your shoulder—and into history—to see that the traffic used to go the other way. For 600 years ago, today's frontier town of Edirne was geographically, spiritually and politically the heart of the vast Ottoman Empire, serving as capital for 91 years.

There are still many fringes of forest and corners of the coast that deserve more attention than they get. At present, they are visited by little more than the waves of the Black Sea, Aegean and Sea of Marmara.

Edirne

A tour of Edirne can be managed comfortably in one day. Most of the principal sights are within walking distance of the main street, Talatpaşa Caddesi.

Crowning everything is the mosque of Selim II, **Selimiye Camii**, whose soaring minarets provide the first, unforgettable glimpse of the Orient for those driving into Turkey from Greece or Bulgaria.

The architect Sinan considered it his masterpiece—and at the age of 86, after designing 500 works of art, he was well qualified to judge. The sultan's grand ideas were fuelled by an almost constant state of inebriation; one of them was to build a mosque that would outshine the fabulous St. Sophia mosque in Istanbul. Sinan excelled himself, with a plan that was astoundingly effective: a dome 31.5 metres (103 ft.) in diameter—bigger than St. Sophia's—accompanied by four slender minarets pointing more than 70 metres (230 ft.) into the sky. Each minaret has three balconies, the sum of which matched Selim's status as 12th Ottoman sultan. Unfortunately, the sultan didn't live to see it completed.

You can enter either from the main courtyard or via the covered market underneath the mosque. Modern-day architects extol the building's virtues of harmony and aesthetics. A remarkable effect of light and space is created by the 999 windows (a thousand, said Selim, would be unsubtle). Even the massive elephant-foot pillars

holding the dome seem delicately poised.

Opposite the fine marble *mihrab*, note the unusual ornate pinewood and marble *şadırvan*, the fountain for washing before prayer which here is for refreshment only. On the front left-hand column as you face the *mihrab*, look for the crude carving of an upside-down tulip. There's a story behind it. The land earmarked for the mosque's construction belonged to an old lady who grew tulips there. Reluctant to have her garden dug up, she refused time and time again to concede the land, until Sinan promised that her generosity would somehow go down in history. So the tulip was carved on the fountain—upside down, because the lady was so contrary.

Nowhere is early Ottoman flower power illustrated so clearly as in the **Old Mosque** *(Eski Cami)*, flanked by two minarets and crowned with nine domes, on the other side of Talatpaşa Caddesi. Work on the mosque started in 1403 and lasted 11 years. Floral patterns can be seen all over the dome decorations, painted in pigments extracted from plants.

Set into the side wall at the right of the simple *mihrab* is a

Sinan's career culminated in the creation of exquisite Selimiye mosque.

piece of the black stone from the Ka'aba, House of God, in Mecca, which Muslims touch for good health, luck, enlightenment or fortune. The exuberantly painted flowers tumbling around it are now faded and the stone is worn into a circular depression almost an inch deep. As well as for its floral significance, the mosque is noted for its samples of calligraphy: you can't miss the exquisite "Allah"—not unlike the letter W—and "Muhammad" at the entrance.

The 14 miniature domes of the **Bedesten Çarşısı** rear up behind the mosque. This covered bazaar once formed part of the mosque complex. The stalls packed into the long stone-arched hall range from the carver of gravestones at one end to the cutter of imitation-fruit soap at the other. Pigeons swoop over the heads of bargain-hunters, their wings beating time to the cries of the stallholders.

Back across Talatpaşa Caddesi, a tea garden offers a break before you tackle the **Three-balconied Mosque** *(Üç Şerefeli Camii)*, recognizable by its four unmatching minarets. The building withstood an earthquake in 1942: see the cracks above the great hexagonal stone pillars. The four marble columns—two either side of the *mihrab* and two fronting the *mimber*—are an unusual feature. They were designed to revolve as long as the mosque stayed on a vertical plane. One of them is stuck now, thanks to the earthquake, but the other three can still be turned by hand.

On the way out, crane your neck to see the 18th-century Baroque restoration designs on the four smaller domes, and don't miss the magnificent entrance doors of carved walnut.

A lighter side to Sinan's design work can be seen in the most famous of Edirne's public baths, the **Sokullu Hamamı.** It was commissioned by the grand vizier of Suleiman the Magnificent, Mehmet Sokullu—a brilliant statesman who handled important matters of state before being murdered two sultans later, on the orders of Murat III. A stray shaft of sunlight pierces the domed roof of the changing rooms. In the bath house itself, you can sweat it out in 45 °C of steamy heat, watching the sun stream through a swirling mist from the diamond- and starshaped ventilation holes in another of the complex's 12 domes.

Sinan's architecture is in evidence again as you run the gauntlet of the **Ali Paşa Çarşısı,** a long tunnel of shops and stalls. The jeans may be from this generation, but perfumes, beads and musical instruments have been selling there for more than 400 years.

Gallipoli *(Gelibolu)*

Many visitors make a pilgrimage to the war graves in Gallipoli. This arm of land lying alongside the Anatolian coast presses the Sea of Marmara into the narrow strait of the Dardanelles (the Hellespont of antique times) before it joins the Aegean. Passenger-vehicle ferries make regular crossings.

Turkey entered World War I on the side of Germany and Austria. Allied operations in the Dardanelles aimed at securing an ice-free passage to Russia to supply arms and open another front. An abortive army-navy assault on Gallipoli, involving French and British forces, was launched in April 1915. On both sides thousands of men lost their lives. In November a freak blizzard accounted for hundreds more deaths, precipitating Allied withdrawal. Australia and New Zealand suffered tremendous losses. The Australian and New Zealand Army Corps (ANZAC) has given its name to Anzac Cove where some of the fiercest fighting occurred.

The whole peninsula is a vast memorial. Each cemetery is signposted; all are perfectly maintained, planted with flowers, scented by hedges of rosemary. Tourist offices in Çanakkale, just across the Dardanelles, and Gelibolu provide a map with each cemetery marked.

AEGEAN COAST

Unmatched for sun-drenched relaxation or for exploring a plethora of ancient sites, Turkey's Aegean coast is endowed with natural beauty. Izmir is a prime point for excursions to the ancient marble ruins. Most holidaymakers, though, choose to take their ease at one of the beach resorts—Çeşme, Kuşadası, Bodrum or Marmaris—and set out from there.

Pergamum *(Bergama)*

Perched above the modern town of Bergama, Pergamum was, at its height, ruled by the Attalids, put into power by Alexander the Great's general, Lysimachus.

Three basic areas attract visitors: the Asclepion, the centre of town and the acropolis.

Above the entrance to the **Asclepion**, one of the most reputed medical centres of the ancient world, was written: "Here death is forbidden by order of the gods". Dedicated to Asclepius, god of healing, rivalling similar centres at Epidauros, Kos and Ephesus, the Asclepion provided hot baths, massage, cures by drinking water from a spring latterly found to be mildly radioactive, and primitive psychiatry. Rational treatment, plus a good measure of faith, reached a peak when Galen (130–200), the "prince of physicians", practised here.

Entry is along a monumental road bordered by columns. A library, theatre and public toilets were provided. The open-roofed "cure centre" was threaded with channels to provide the therapeutic sound of running water for patients; afterwards their dreams were analyzed for diagnosis.

The remains of the city of the Attalids rise on a series of artificial terraces. See the ruins of the **Pergamene library**, near the Temple of Athena, goddess of learning. The Attalids loved books and managed by fair means and foul to build up a collection of some 200,000 manuscripts. When Alexandria's library was destroyed by fire, Antony gave Cleopatra all Pergamum's books.

The biggest building on the acropolis is the **Trajaneum**, erected in the 2nd century for the deified Roman emperors, Trajan and Hadrian.

Set in the hillside, the **theatre** is a tighter half-moon shape than most, and impressively steep. East Berlin's Pergamum Museum was the recipient of a remarkable frieze—one of the finest existing examples of Hellenistic sculpture, representing the Battle of the Gods and the Giants—which enhanced the nearby Altar of Zeus, built to commemorate the defeat of the Gauls in 190 B.C. Other temples, gymnasia, fountains, agoras, palaces and houses all attest to the artistic and economic achievements of Pergamum.

Many examples of votive offerings to Asclepius are in the **Bergama Museum**, along with other finds from the area and Turkish-Islamic objects.

Izmir and Environs

This sparkling city, still often known by its Greek name of Smyrna, is well served by air, land and sea. In the summer there's a regular overnight ferry from Istanbul with a range of cabin and deck accommodation. If you're driving from the north, detour to the superb beach villages of Yeni Foça and Eski Foça. The latter is the site of ancient Phocaea, whose mariners were described by Herodotus as "the pioneer navigators of the Greeks". They founded dozens of colonies, one of which, Massilia, became Marseilles. By road or sea you'll be treated to a memorable view of Turkey's third largest metropolis, spread

Konak Square, the heart of downtown Izmir.

around the shores of a beautiful bay.

An Aeolian colony was established north of the bay in the 10th century B.C., afterwards replaced by Ionians, also from the Greek mainland. The poet Homer, who was probably born in Smyrna, belonged to this brilliant civilization. Later, Alexander the Great visited and refounded the city around Mount Pagus as the result of a dream he had there. When the Ottoman Turks arrived, they allowed Europeans to install trading stations, and Izmir grew wealthy handling merchandise from the interior, including Smyrna figs and Turkish tobacco. It prospered as a Levantine port until almost completely destroyed by fire in 1922, at the close of the Greek-Turkish war. Rebuilt on the former site, just where Alexander wanted it, today's city of 800,000 people is as animated as ever, but almost no trace remains of its past.

From the port a broad boulevard, Atatürk Caddesi, popularly called the Kordon, stretches through the heart of town. Horses decked with blue and orange pompoms draw spanking *faytons* for a sightseeing tour, taking in the south-east headquarters of NATO, Cumhuriyet Meydanı (Republic Square) with its equestrian statue of Atatürk, and finishing at Konak Square. The tiny mosque, Konak Camii, was built in 1756; nearby is the city's symbol, a curlicued clock-tower dating from 1901. The tourist office is here, and it's also the starting-point for municipal buses.

Take the overhead bridge to the **bazaar,** less exciting than Istanbul's but jam-packed with goods, the whole paraphernalia of daily living. It's a great deal more wide-awake than the Roman marketplace or **agora,** built in the 2nd century, now an idyllic retreat of bleached grass where lizards bask in the sun. There are remains of a colonnade. Statues of gods are grouped in reduced circumstances in the north-west corner, but the best finds have been removed to the **Archaeo-logical Museum** *(Arkeoloji Müzesi)* in the Culture Park.

Kadifekale ("the Velvet Castle"), Izmir's flat-topped guardian, is Mount Pagus of antiquity. The view is exceptionally fine over the agora and Konak Square to the bay, where ferries ply across blue water to the opposite shore.

At night, from out in the bay, the city's lights flicker like a giant, glittering tiara.

Sardis

Sardis, one-time capital of Lydia, used to be the wealthiest city in the world. Logically enough, the Lydians invented coined money, most of it stamped with a lion's head, the royal emblem of the city. Under Croesus, the last king (560–546 B.C.), coins of pure gold and silver were minted. The gold was washed down by the River Pactolus; the Greek historian Herodotus relates that specks of the precious metal were caught in the fleece of sheepskins spread in the shallows, giving rise to the legend of the Golden Fleece. Sardis was overrun by the Persians, terminating the reign of Croesus and the Lydian monarchy.

Today's village of Sart stands near the ruins. Most imposing is the **Temple of Artemis**, an enormous structure boasting some of the finest Ionic capitals ever excavated. A 5th-century

Byzantine church leans up against it. Above, a fairly tough climb away, is the acropolis.

Across the highway from the temple, a majestic 3rd-century synagogue has been restored with American funds, as have remains of shops outside the walls. These were part of a complex which included the gymnasium, the whole a handsome example of Roman architecture.

Manisa

Nearby Manisa, formerly Magnesia ad Sipylum, was capital of the Byzantine Empire for a brief period in the 13th century, when the emperor withdrew here to escape from the Crusaders. Originating from Magnesia in Northern Greece, early inhabitants claimed to be the first Greeks in Asia. Classical ruins are almost non-existent but there are several fine Ottoman religious buildings, one of which has been converted into a museum.

Spring and summer deck the slopes of Mount Sipylus with myriad wild flowers—violets, cyclamen in thousands, hyacinths and the Sipylus tulip, with pointed flame-coloured petals, which provided the original bulbs for this favourite flower of Ottoman times and subsequently for the Dutch tulip industry. At the foot of the mountain there's a bas-relief of Cybele, the Anatolian mother-goddess.

Colophon

This little site is accessible by road via the town of Değirmendere, south of Izmir. Colophonians were extremely wealthy in their time; they dressed in purple robes and smothered themselves in perfume to frequent the marketplace. This extravagance, combined with gourmandizing habits, attracted the criticism of early historians and brought about the city's downfall. In time Colophon merged with Notium, which became known as New Colophon. The ruins are scanty in both places. **Claros** was not a city but the site of a temple and oracle of Apollo, whose proximity provided the source of Colophon's wealth. The temple has been excavated but is practically covered by river water.

Teos is not a major destination, but it's such a thoroughly delightful spot that it's worth a visit. Turn off at Seferihisar for the village of Sığaçık and drive through orange groves towards the island-studded bay. You'll feel as though you've found *your* archaeological site. Here there are no ticket offices, no souvenirs and almost certainly no other visitors. Appropriate gestures in the local grocery will unearth a friendly villager quite prepared to meander with you through the ruins. The old agora is a melon field; skyblue convolvulus twines among blocks of the bluish Teian marble-like limestone still quarried near Seferihisar. For full enjoyment, bring a picnic. The road continues to the sea.

The Aegean coast is a paradise, for fishermen and homemakers alike.

Çeşme

The forked peninsula thrusting west from Izmir has a real jewel in the little town of Çeşme.

The pristine whitewash on the houses is all the more startling when the *imbat*, an invigorating sea breeze, blows, setting coloured carpets flapping against shop balconies. But the **beaches** are the main attraction. Golden Dolphin Holiday Village has one

of Turkey's rare casinos and there are many other hotels around the Bay of Boyalik with, for good measure, a thermal pool in the sea at Ilıca. There's motel, bungalow and *pansiyon* accommodation too, often offering thermal facilities.

There are few monuments—which may well come as a relief. Çeşme does have its 14th-century Genoese fort, a small one, and a rather grand caravanserai alongside. Some 22 kilometres (14 mi.) away, Ildır is the site of the ancient city of Erythrae, but even there the beautiful situation takes precedence over the ruins.

Kuşadası and Environs

Some of the privileged storks of this world have their nests on old stone columns along the Izmir-Selçuk road which leads on to

*Try out the acoustics of Ephesus'
Great Theatre—a voice from the
stage can be heard in the top row.*

Kuşadası. The name, meaning
"Island of Birds", refers to a
small promontory. Apart from
a small fort on Güvercin Adası
and a 17th-century caravanserai
converted into an hotel, ruins
are thin on the ground in the
Kuşadası area itself, which is
dedicated to the good life of

boating and bronzing. There
could be no more pleasant spot
for doing just those things,
blessed as it is with crystalline
water, golden sand and fish that
almost pop out of the sea onto
the plate. But when thoughts do
turn to exploring further than the
next palm tree, there's plenty of
history nearby and some left
over.

One of the best-preserved and
most-visited of all the Aegean

from the town of Selçuk to one of the greatest of ancient cities. Founded before the 10th century B.C. by Ionian Greeks (who gave this area of coast its old name), it was ruled in turn by Croesus, king of Lydia, Cyrus, king of Persia and the Attalids, kings of Pergamum. The last Attalid bequeathed Ephesus to Rome. At its height there were 200,000 inhabitants. Camel caravans brought the exotic treasures of the East; Greece, to the west, supplied suitable gods for worship. Queen of them all was Artemis (Diana), whose personality of virgin huntress merged with the role of an Anatolian fertility goddess, Cybele. The great Temple of Artemis, one of the Seven Wonders of the World, was erected in her honour. Intellectually, spiritually and commercially, this was one of the most splendid cities ever known. But the greatness of Ephesus was linked to its port. When the harbour silted up in the 3rd century, the city went into a decline. The site was rediscovered in 1869 by a British engineer-archaeologist after six years' searching. Most of what you see belongs to the Roman imperial period.

Tours usually begin at the Magnesian Gate. The well-preserved **odeum** is here, and next to it the **prytaneum**, or town hall, where the two statues of Artemis in the Ephesus museum were

cities, Ephesus, lies 17 kilometres (10½ mi.) inland. Many other remains dot the countryside, for this region is Ionia, famous in ancient times for the softness of its landscape, the kindness of its climate, the lushness of its valleys. It vies with Greece itself for numbers of monuments.

Ephesus *(Efes)*

An avenue bordered by mulberry trees takes you within minutes

81

found. Walk down the marble street called Curetes Way. The Temple of Domitian and the marvellously restored Temple of Hadrian were dedicated to the emperors-cum-gods. The adjoining Baths of Scolastica were a large complex including a brothel, with its entrance at the south corner of Marble Street. Keep an eye out for the signs carved into a paving-stone indicating the way.

The **Library of Celsus**, a miracle of restoration, was built in the 2nd century by a Roman consul as memorial and tomb for his father. Air channels ran behind the niches storing the manuscripts, to control humidity.

The **Great Theatre**, set with its back to Mount Pion, could seat 25,000 people. Drama and music fans still crowd into the theatre each spring during a local festival.

The **Arcadian Way** advances grandly from the theatre to the port. Behind the **gymnasium** are the **Twin Churches of Mary**. The original Roman basilica was used as a commercial building, then transformed into a church on whose ruins two later churches were raised.

A charming legend is attached

Ice-blue pools with frosty trimmings make for swimming with a difference at Pamukkale.

to the **Cave of the Seven Sleepers**, between Ephesus and Selçuk at the foot of Mount Pion, telling of persecuted Christian lads who slept here for two centuries, then awoke to find Christianity the state religion.

The small town of **Selçuk** has several noteworthy monuments. The 6th-century **Basilica of St. John** marks the spot where the Apostle spent his last years and died. Down the hill is **Isa Bey Mosque** (1375). The daunting fortress atop the hill dates from Byzantine times. Don't miss the museum, even if it's only to see the two statues of Artemis.

The **Virgin Mary's House** *(Meryemana)* lies outside the town on what used to be known as Mount Coressos (now Bülbüldağı). Here Mary is thought to have spent her last days. Foundations of the present house seem to be 1st century, and the location was discovered some 100 years ago through the visions of a German woman, Catherine Emmerich. It's long been a place of pilgrimage.

Inland to Pamukkale

You can take a day trip to Pamukkale from Kuşadası or Izmir, but it's tiring. Try instead to stay overnight and enjoy the thermal pools, also to visit Aphrodisias, not the most publicized but one of the best of all the ancient sites.

The road runs through the rich valley of the river the Greeks knew as the Maeander.

Turn off past Kuyucak for **Aphrodisias,** 38 kilometres (23 mi.) away. In the distance hovers Baba Dağı, "Father's Mountain", with snow folded in the ridges even in midsummer. The Aphrodisias site is at the village of Geyre, and the museum is well worth a visit for cult statues of Aphrodite, discreetly gowned and looking particularly well-behaved for a goddess of love.

Not much remains of her temple, but the **stadium** is enormous, possibly the finest in the ancient world, with a length of 228 metres (748 ft.) and seating capacity for 30,000, still put to use at festival time.

The recently excavated theatre is outclassed for charm by a small **odeum** with a semicircular pool. It's the sort of place you feel Aphrodite would have chosen herself: dragonflies hover above waterlilies, doves coo in the bushes and petals from wild pomegranate trees drop in scarlet showers onto white marble.

The main highway proceeds past a turnoff to Laodicea. Hold your breath from here on because across the plain, pillared by stalactites, shining like an alabaster palace, towers Pamukkale, the **Cotton Castle**. Hot thermal springs pouring from Çal Dağı have created this limestone formation of scalloped basins and cascading water, looking for all the world as though carved out of ice and cloud by some angelic hand.

Above it stood Hieropolis, the "Holy City", named for its quantity of temples; nowadays they are replaced by hotels, where you can swim in natural warm pools. For a unique experience visit the Turizm Hotel enclosing the **Sacred Pool**, the realm of watery deities. Buoyant water floats you above fluted marble and broken Corinthian capitals. Cedars and oleanders shade the source of the spring.

The remains of Hieropolis include the Roman baths, the theatre and a big necropolis which is thought to contain the tomb of the Apostle Philip. Before returning to the coast visit **Ak Han**, a 13th-century Seljuk caravanserai.

Other Sites

The Ionian coast between Kuşadası and Bodrum has a cluster of three major sites which can be seen in one day.

Priene, once one of the most active ports in the Ionian Confederation, now stands several miles inland as a result of the silting up of the Maeander River. In spite of Roman alterations it's basically an ancient Greek city, particularly interesting for its grid layout.

The big **Temple of Athena** retains several of its Ionic columns. It was still being built when Alexander the Great arrived in 334 B.C., and he paid for its completion. The theatre, a temple to Zeus and the bouleterion ("Council House") are other main buildings; a fairly short climb brings you to the Sanctuary of Demeter and Kore (Persephone), the oldest of the holy places in Priene.

Miletus (or Milet) today is set above melancholy marshes where frogs croak at nightfall, seeming to mourn the downfall of this erstwhile stronghold of maritime power, one of the principal ports and centres of the Greek world. In the 8th and 7th centuries B.C. Miletus established almost 100 colonies. The landscape has completely changed over the years; many of the ruins are subjected to regular flooding, but the Graeco-Roman theatre is superb.

Didyma (Didim) has only one monument, a Temple to Apollo. No city ever stood here, just this colossal temple, one of the largest and most elegant of ancient times, renowned for its oracle. When the Persians under Darius destroyed Miletus in 494 B.C. they destroyed Didyma's temple, too. For several centuries it was under reconstruction but was never completed—you'll see that some of the columns have been left unfluted.

Bodrum

Bodrum is set against an unbelievably blue sea. The flat-roofed, square-built houses are almost blinding under the hot sun, their white walls festooned with great clusters of purple bougainvillea. Luxurious yachts crowd the marina, an international crowd enlivens the streets and keeps the night young with music and dancing. It's all easy-going, fun-loving, with a touch of cosmopolitan Bohemia: the St. Tropez of Turkey.

Bodrum's old name is Halicarnassus, capital of the former region of Caria. Herodotus, the "Father of History", was born here. Mausolus was the most famous ruler; his mausoleum (the word comes from his name) was one of the Seven Wonders of the World.

Apart from remains of the theatre and sections of the city wall, the only surviving ancient monument is the **mausoleum,** and there's not much left of that. The area where it stood is an open-air museum. Mausolus started building it himself around 355 B.C.

Destroyed by earthquake, the mausoleum was quarried by the Knights of St. John to help build the 15th-century **Castle of St. Peter** which still dominates today's port and city. Now an amazing museum, the stupendous fortress was constructed when the Knights were forced out of Smyrna by Tamerlane.

The castle towers represent the

Medieval melodies echo from the grey stones of Bodrum's castle.

various tongues under which the knights were grouped: hence there is an English, French, German and Italian Tower, plus the Serpentine Tower.

There's a tremendous view from the top of the towers, and you'll be able to look down into the boatyards of Bodrum, where many a prestige yacht is still built according to the centuries-old traditions of the region.

Bodrum is not the spot for swimming but there is no lack of paradisal beaches in the area.

Soft and creamy, hard and chunky: local cheese for every taste in Bodrum market.

Boat tours make a day trip, leaving Bodrum at 9–10 a.m., visiting beaches all the way to Karaincir, and returning at about 6 p.m.

The ancient site of **Knidos** across the bay on the Marmaris peninsula can be visited by boat on a day trip. With more time and expense, you can arrange a trip in the Gulf of Gökova, between Bodrum and Marmaris. It really is a boatman's dream—uninhabited islands, fish aplenty, forested shorelines and sandy beaches.

Kos lies off the coast of Bodrum; there's a regular ferry service to this Greek island.

Marmaris

Translucent waters and a shoreline edged with dark conifers and contrasting pink oleanders give this town a peaceful, picturesque air. Amusing carriages pulled by miniature tractors take you off to the nearby beaches; boats ferry passengers around the bay to more dramatically beautiful spots, for this is one of the most indented areas of the whole coast. The Greek island of Rhodes is a 3-hour trip away by ferry. The town is served by Dalaman Airport, some 100 kilometres (62 mi.) away.

There's little to remind you that Marmaris is ancient Physcus, belonging to the Carian kingdom. The fort is 16th-century. No ruins, but pleasant little Turkish houses, shops still managing to stock an astonishing quantity of antiques—from stilted bath-clogs to brass coffee-grinders—and enough restaurants and discos to keep you happily occupied when the sun goes down. The harbour is the centre of activity, where the atmosphere is noisy and cheerful. It's a great place for families, with the added advantage that you can swim from early June to the last days of September.

And it's here that the Aegean meets the Mediterranean, with the long, pine-laden peninsula as dividing-line. To its west is the fishing village of Datça.

MEDITERRANEAN COAST

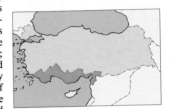

The craggy coastline of Turkey's southern shore is an unending succession of pleasant surprises —perfumed pine forests, banana palms bending heavy with fruit, sophisticated marinas, surfboarding galore and the endless vista of the turquoise-blue Mediterranean.

All along the winding shoreline unfolds dramatic mountain scenery, topped by the southern Taurus mountains that faithfully follow the Mediterranean, keeping the Anatolian plain at a safe distance. The sliver of snow at the top is the closest thing to winter that you'll see.

The region is steeped in history: Lycia, land of the tombs; the plain of Pamphylia; and Cilicia. Here, the initiation into ancient ruins is a painless and relaxing affair. Just take a picnic and swimming gear.

Fethiye to Phaselis

No matter how hard it tries, **Fethiye** doesn't manage the air of urbanity of its big-marina neighbour, Marmaris. The little town turns away from the open sea into the shelter of a natural harbour, enjoying gently reflecting ripples. At night, the strains of folk music drift along the sea front; in the morning, the mist rises over a peaceful bay decorated with islands.

Fethiye was once known as Telmessos. Ancient Lycian tombs appear where you would least expect them, in the middle of town. Walk up to the cliffs to see the imposing **rock tombs** of the more important personalities cut deep into the surface, framed with Ionic columns and their façades representing the wooden buildings of the time. An inscription on one reveals it as the tomb of King Amyntas, from the 4th century B.C. The ruined castle you can see was built during the Crusades by the Knights of St. John.

Main attraction is **Ölü Deniz,** the silvery tongue of land that transforms a mile-long beach into an idyllic lagoon. Sheltered swimming, pine-shaded sands and instant accommodation—from motels to camping—draw

Crystal-clear water is guaranteed at Ölü Deniz—yachts are kept out of the lagoon.

floods of visitors and leave Fethiye thankful for the respite. *Dolmuş* mini-buses run a regular service to the lagoon, 15 minutes away. One relaxing diversion is to hire a boat and explore the bay *(körfezi)* of Belceğiz, particularly the Byzantine ruins on the island of **Gemile,** which include sunken buildings from the village of Aya Nikola.

Fethiye's own beach, **Çalış** —10 minutes by *dolmuş*—boasts restaurants, discotheques and camping places. From it, you look out on to **Şövalye,** one of the "Dozen Islands" that adorn the Gulf of Fethiye, 20 minutes by boat. About 13 kilometres (8 mi.) north, the bays of Katrancı and Günlük, the latter sometimes referred to as **Küçük Kargı,** are both equipped with bathing huts and showers.

From Dalyan, west of Fethiye, you can hire a boat for a cruise to the ruins of **Caunus,** an important Carian city in 400 B.C. As Caunus was on the border with Lycia, the ruins reflect both cultures. The theatre is well preserved, and you can also see remains of the acropolis. But the most interesting are the Lycian tombs, carved high in the rock face. The trip to the ruins and back takes about three hours.

The site of **Xanthos** boasts famous Lycian tombs once decorated with reliefs, now replaced by plaster casts.

Kalkan and Kaş

East of Fethiye, the pretty fishing port of **Kalkan** nestles snugly in the cliffs overlooking a bay. There are few sightseeing attractions—for which the townspeople are grateful—but close by are several sea caves accessible by motor boat. The main one is called the Blue Grotto. While it may not live up to its famous namesake in Capri, the scenery further round more than matches the splendour of southern Italy. As you are poised almost 3,000 feet above Kaş, the view of the islands and a ribbon of mainland snaking out to sea is breathtaking.

Some 2,500 years ago, **Kaş** was the thriving Lycian port of Antiphellos. Nowadays it's coming back into fashion, aided by an uncrowded harbour setting enhanced by white-painted stone buildings. An atmosphere of lively informality prevails, and the tree-shaded cafés do a brisk trade all day. The Hellenistic theatre, relatively sound and encircled by olive trees, was once the focal point of the town's leisure activities, but now that has moved with the times to the beaches. On the eastern side of Kaş you can see Lycian **rock tombs** hewn out of the cliffs; one sarcophagus stands offshore in half-submerged isolation.

Boat trips are organized to the island of **Kekova**, 29 kilometres (18 mi.) away, to see Byzantine church ruins and underwater sarcophagi. The 8-hour journey takes in lunch at the mainland village of **Üçağız**, where an acropolis contains many more tombs. Nearby **Kale** has a theatre in the remains of a castle.

The coastline is beautiful, but rugged. Two possibilities for swimming are **Patara**, just outside Kalkan, and **Kaputaş**, a tiny cove about 20 kilometres (12 mi.) beyond Kaş. The road turns sharply, hugging the cliff as it crosses a ravine from which steps lead to the cove. Be careful if driving.

Demre

A precipitous mountain road leads to the tumbledown town of Demre, crowded with rickety greenhouses stuffed full of tomatoes, aubergines and other vegetables. Apart from being a miracle of market gardening in such barren surroundings, Demre is the home of St. Nicholas, patron saint of children. St. Nicholas was born at Patara in the 4th century A.D., but he served as bishop of the Lycian city of Myra, around which Demre has developed.

Rock tombs at Demre,
a familiar feature
of this part of the coast.

In a small shaded garden outside the **Church of Father Christmas** *(Noel Baba Kilisesi)* stands a black-painted fibreglass statue of the bearded bishop, wearing his traditional robes, carrying a sack full of presents and surrounded by expectant children. An aisle of the Byzantine church—constructed after the death of St. Nicholas—contains the tomb from which his remains were stolen in 1087 by Italian merchants from Bari. They were in such a hurry that they left some pieces of bone, duly preserved in the museum at Antalya. Note discreetly the pillar with a Greek inscription, replaced upside down during restoration.

Each year, Demre holds a symposium and festival with music, dancing and present-giving to commemorate the anniversary of the bishop's death on December 6th.

A 15-minute walk away, past houses that look even less stable than the greenhouses, are the **rock tombs** of Myra. As you cross an irrigation ditch, look out for a slab of stone almost hidden by the bushes, bearing three theatre masks in relief, from Myra's splendid Roman **amphitheatre.** The tombs are cut neatly above, and next to, one another with the economy of space of a multi-storey block of flats.

Olympos

Armed with a bag of thirst-quenching oranges from the fishing village of Finike, ancient Phoenicus, you can drive to the ruins of Olympos in less than an

---

Southern Santa

Believe it or not, Father Christmas was born in the south of Turkey, far from the icy wastes of Lapland.

St. Nicholas gained a reputation for generosity as Bishop of Myra, in the 4th century B.C. A former city dignitary had fallen on hard times and had no money to marry off his eldest daughter. The bishop overheard one of her sisters offering to sell herself to raise a dowry. So he secretly threw a bag of gold through a window of their home. He repeated the gesture on two further occasions, enabling all three girls to be married.

Nicholas became one of the most popular saints in Christendom; he was adopted as patron saint of scholars, sailors, merchants and pawnbrokers—their emblem of three golden balls was inspired by the three bags of gold. In many European countries, his feast-day, the 6th December, is celebrated by someone dressing in a bishop's costume and distributing gifts to children. The custom was introduced to England from Germany in the early years of Victoria's reign, adding another dimension to Christmas festivities.

hour. A turn-off takes you the last 11 kilometres (7 mi.) to the site, set at the mouth of a shallow river that brought the city fresh water and trading prosperity, making it a significant member of the Lycian League around 100 B.C. Its fortunes waned rapidly after becoming a pillaging ground for pirates, who amused themselves at the expense of local inhabitants by carrying out sacrifices and other rituals for the Persian god of light, Mithras.

Not much remains of the city's **temple** except a decorated doorway and part of the wall. A statue base is dedicated to Emperor Marcus Aurelius, around 100 years after the area was brought under Roman control. Several of the 200 tombs in the **necropolis**—many of them ornate vaulted chambers—carry fortune-telling oracles. The enquirer, usually seeking advice about a proposed journey, would draw a letter of the alphabet. He might just as well have tossed a coin, for the 24 different answers—written in verse form and each beginning with a different letter of the alphabet—can be summed up as either "Stay at home" or "Go ahead".

Look around from the wide shingle beach at the 2,377-metre (7,800-ft.) Mt. Olympos (Tahtalı Dağ), from which the city's name came. The mountain is associated with a flame, one

that has been burning since time immemorial, the famous **Yanar**. It's a natural gas outlet; if extinguished, the flame promptly re-ignites a few seconds later. A stiff walk north-west of the ruins takes you up to this phenomenon which has fascinated historians and travellers for centuries. It probably gave rise to the myth of the Chimaera, the fire-breathing beast part serpent, part goat and part lion slain by the hero Bellerophon. The ruins scattered around the fire are all that remains of a sanctuary built for Hephaestos, the god of fire (the Romans knew him as Vulcan).

Phaselis

A few kilometres further along the Antalya road, just after Tekirova, a thickly wooded headland almost conceals the ruins of Phaselis, at its height a keen trading port famous for its rose perfume. The city was founded by a group of colonists from Rhodes who reportedly arrived in 690 B.C. and persuaded the resident shepherd to part with his land for some dried fish. Phaselis suffered badly at the hands of the same pirates who terrorized Olympos, and later faded into obscurity.

A stony track leads down through pine trees to the **aqueduct** that brought water to the city from a spring. Apart from

95

the Hellenistic walls of a fortified settlement north of the aqueduct, the remains are Roman and Byzantine. Walk on to a picturesque clearing at the edge of the sea, ideal for picnics. The quinqueremes have long gone, but as many cabin cruisers and sailing boats seeking the flame of Olympos anchor here overnight. Of the three ancient harbours, the middle one has silted up obligingly to provide perfect swimming. Alexander the Great marched along the beach towards Perge, for his next conquest, after arriving here in 333 B.C. The people of Phaselis welcomed him with open arms and a golden crown.

Antalya to Side

The clusters of Roman-candle street lamps along a sweeping palm-lined boulevard tell you that **Antalya** is more than just a holiday resort. The sprawl of white concrete attests to the city's fame as a tourist paradise; the picturesque old town shows its chequered history.

Antalya's success story has been helped as much by what it lacks as by what it has: no railway link with inland cities, no pollution-related industry and no winter to speak of. Despite its sleepy position in a natural harbour, Antalya is a busy community with a population of a quarter of a million people, mainly oc-cupied with the region's agricultural and farming output.

Miles of beaches spread either side of the city. The coastal stretch to the east is dotted with coves, some tucked far below the cliffs. The quietest beach is **Lara**, a tempting expanse of sand. A chorus of croaking bullfrogs from the marshes accompanies evening traffic along the road into town. To the west, pebbly **Konyaaltı** beach curves round to the pine sands opposite a triangular-shaped rock offshore known as Mouse Island.

One of Antalya's best landmarks—and its oldest example of Seljuk architecture—is the **Grooved Minaret** (Yivli Minare), an unusual arrangement of eight half-cylinders once complete with blue porcelain tiles. It was built in the 13th century by the Seljuk sultan Alaettin Keykubat.

Hadrian's Gate (Hadrianus Kapısı) on the eastern wall of the old town, marks a visit by Emperor Hadrian in A.D. 130. White marble pillars grace the three arches, which are flanked by two rectangular Roman towers, one with Seljuk additions.

The mosque of the **Truncated Minaret** (Kesik Minare) was originally a Byzantine church, re-

Hadrian's Gate at Antalya has been restored to its former elegance.

stored many times since the 5th century. The minaret acquired its name when it was decapitated by lightning during a storm.

Further round, the **Hıdırlık Kulesi,** a squat tower, forms part of the city fortifications. Its exact function is not clear, but the layout has prompted speculation that it was originally built as the tomb of an influential Roman in the 2nd century A.D.

Quaint narrow streets and alleyways retain a 17th-century Ottoman charm as they lead through the old town, now a preservation area, to the inner **harbour.** Yachts bob gently in the shade of the walls built more than 2,000 years ago when the Pergamene king Attalus II founded the port, naming it Attaleia after himself.

Flowers waft a fragrance in the **City Park** (Karaali Parkı) further down Atatürk Caddesi. Through the palm trees, the mountains on the opposite side of the bay make a restful backdrop for a picnic break from sightseeing.

Antalya's **Archaeological Museum** (Arkeoloji Müzesi), on the west of town, houses a comprehensive selection of exhibits from the Palaeolithic Age. Mosaics from Xanthos include one depicting a boar hunt from the 4th–5th centuries A.D. The remaining bones of St. Nicholas are also kept here.

Termessos

Despite their warlike tendencies—or perhaps because of them—the people of Termessos enjoyed special relations with Rome in the 2nd century B.C. A friendship treaty effectively guaranteed them independence of Roman rule and excluded the billeting of Roman soldiers in the city. The Termessians—who had few allies and didn't need them anyway—were not very impressed. They went on to make their own currency, pointedly declining to include the customary Head of the Emperor.

The remains of Termessos are perched high up on a rocky promontory, 34 kilometres (21 mi.) inland, north-west of Antalya. The **theatre,** 1,067 metres (3,500 ft.) above the Pamphylian plain, offered a view which must have rivalled any spectacle on the stage for the 5,000 members of the audience. The **odeum,** close by, was the local hall of fame for sportsmen, whose main interest was wrestling. Other events included running races, races in armour and, even on a mountain, horse racing. The dice oracle reappears (see p. 95) inscribed on a gateway along what was once called King's Street. This time the verses are numbered, corresponding to the throws of five four-sided dice.

A second street lined with shops had about 50 columns on

each side with statues in front and between them erected in honour of sportsmen and city officials. The statues have all gone, but you can still decipher inscriptions on the bases.

Among the tangle of trees and boulders in the upper part of the city is the **necropolis,** with dozens of rock tombs and others cut from stone. Most carry an inscribed curse on grave robbers, together with a posthumous warning that anyone disturbing the occupier's tomb will have a hefty fine to pay. It seems that little notice was taken of the threats: the tomb claiming the highest fine has been moved aside and two others put in its place.

Perge

A 20-minute drive east from Antalya will take you to the ancient site of Perge. The turn-off, at Aksu, leads straight to the **theatre,** a formidable combination of Greek and Roman elements. The planning shows unusual sophistication in the configuration of the parodoi and vomitoria, two forms of passageway, which made for speedy seating of the 14,000 spectators. The Romans added an arcaded gallery, and a nymphaeum was built against the outer wall for the water supply. Look for the fine reliefs showing the birth of Dionysus, as he is taken from the thigh of his father Zeus with that admirable disregard for the laws of biology of which only the gods were capable.

The **stadium,** which once echoed to the roar of 15,000 spectators, is still in good condition, although the ornamental entrance to the 234-metre (770-ft.) arena is missing. Some of the arched chambers around it were Roman shops; in several of them you can make out the names of shopkeepers.

You need an hour to examine the ruins. A small, tree-shaded stand provides welcome refreshment, with cold drinks and an escape from the sun.

Aspendos

The pride of Aspendos is its Roman theatre, generally accepted as being one of the best preserved in the world. The site is an effortless 49 kilometres (30 mi.) from Antalya, the last mile following in part the Köprü stream (look back at the quaint humpback bridge built by the Seljuks). The theatre spoils you for anything else, so it is a good idea to look at the other ruins first.

The theatre building backs on to the first of two hills, with the main part of the city—including basilica, market hall and agora —occupying the second. Bridging the half-mile-wide plain below you can see the remains of the **aqueduct**—much more

sophisticated than usual, thanks to a special grant received in the 2nd century A.D. Water was piped under pressure from the mountains. Near the stadium, many tombs and funeral monuments have been dug up. The official ones went to Antalya's museum. The others found their way to the neighbouring village of Belkis, where enterprising villagers installed them as entrance steps to their homes.

When it was built in the 2nd century A.D., the **theatre** comfortably accommodated more than 15,000 people. Some of them have their names carved into the back of the seats. An inner staircase leads up to the halfway point, the diazoma—a wide, semi-circular aisle separating the 40 rows of seats into upper and lower sections. The theatre has been restored, but in places the work is more colourful than convincing.

The very completeness of the theatre is a novelty. Its remarkable acoustics enable you to hear from the top floor a muttered conversation at stage level, mainly because the back wall is still standing. This was enhanced at one time by a wooden roof that sloped over the stage. From the top of the theatre, the plain

In Perge, the moon goddess Artemis is represented by an ornate stone relief.

stretches past like a deserted runway, attracting no more than the occasional passing stork. The fields beyond were a favourite place of meditation for one of the world's early environmentalists, Diodorus—a follower of the Cynic movement who went around Aspendos longhaired, barefoot and unwashed, spurning material pleasures for the simple life.

Manavgat

For a relaxing break from ruin-visiting, stop off at Manavgat, famed for its waterfall. You'll have to revise your ideas on geography: many people might not even rate Manavgat Falls as a respectable rapids. But it has an enduring charm that is hard to beat.

The falls are just outside the small village, transformed over the past 20 years into a prosperous tourist town of 30,000. The waterfall *(Şelale)* remains unspoilt. An endless stream of visitors crosses the footbridge to a partly paved stretch of the river bank. Under the trees, tables and chairs are laid out with casual abandon wherever a space presents itself, teetering as close to the swirling waters as possible.

The audience is appreciative as two forks of the river meet around an island and pour smoothly over what, to be brutally frank, is not much more than a 3-foot drop. But nobody minds. The roar is convincing and a liberal dose of *rakı* discourages comparison-making. Turkish tea, ice cream and kebab are also the order of the day, and in case the background babble of cheerful confusion isn't loud enough, amplifiers help project the combined vocal and instrumental output of a Turkish folk group. What the place lacks in dramatic effect, it more than makes up for in atmosphere.

Side

A road festooned with advertisement boards takes you enthusiastically the 3 kilometres from Manavgat to Side, that rare but delightful combination of ancient and modern—a 2,500-year-old city and holiday resort rolled into one. Kebab stands, cafés and souvenir-sellers do a roaring trade in the crowded streets of today's Selimiye, fitted like a jigsaw piece into the tiny headland.

Today's sought-after sands were not much help in the days of the Lydians, who had the mammoth task of building an artificial harbour and an even greater job of keeping it navigable. Side was the only port in the region until the Pergamene king Attalus II established Attaleia, modern-day Antalya. Coins of Side carried the pomegranate,

a popular symbol of fertility, from which the city's name derived.

Side's Hellenistic **theatre**, one of the biggest in the region, has an enviable setting close to the shore. It is turned slightly away from the water, following the only natural incline, into which the seating is traditionally built. Since this alone was not high enough, a vaulted building had to be constructed for support. The position of the seating had the added advantage of keeping 17,000 pairs of eyes fixed firmly on the acting and not on the tempting horizon.

An aqueduct brought water from the Manavgat river, almost 32 kilometres (20 mi.) away, to the **nymphaeum**, one of the largest along the coast. The decoration included the dolphins and fish reliefs that characterize Roman fresh-water installations, but much of it has disappeared.

Many of the statues and sarcophagi retrieved from the ruins can be seen in Side's **museum**, originally the Roman baths.

Alanya to Tarsus

The mighty rock juts out indomitably into the sea. Crenellated ramparts are everywhere. But beyond the defences, the town's beleaguered air dissolves into a smile: palm trees, smart hotels and *faytons* have you almost believing you're on the Riviera.

The silhouette of a minaret jolts you out of the *belle époque* and back into the Orient. This memorable landmark is effectively the midway point of Turkey's playboy coast, a mecca for windsurfing and swimming.

If **Alanya** looks belligerent, it's the result of centuries of experience. Antiochus III of Syria found it the only coastal city he was unable to capture. The impregnability later made it a natural bolthole for pirates until they were routed in a sea battle by Pompey. Even when Mark Antony made a present of Alanya to Cleopatra, she had her eye more on the rich source of cedar wood for warships than on the romance of the beaches. Sultan Alaettin Keykubat managed to take the city only because the Armenian governor was ready to give way. In 17th-century Ottoman Turkey, the townspeople were licensed to shoot on sight anyone who happened to be a Frank, Armenian or Jew (Greeks were allowed to settle in their own areas).

These days the welcome is distinctly warmer, and the main target of the invading hordes is the soft underbelly of sand lining Alanya's bay.

The octagonal **Red Tower** *(Kızıl Kule)* is a satisfyingly complete example of Seljuk defensive thinking, right down to the openings for dousing attackers with boiling liquids. Oil was favourite—there was little enough water for drinking, let alone throwing away. The 400 open storage tanks were a must, since it doesn't often rain in southern Turkey.

From there, you can see the **Tersane** or dockyard, a fascinating relic of Seljuk naval power. Just beyond is the **Tophane** (arsenal), joined to the city walls, from which the dockyard was defended. The walls lead up to the **Inner Castle** *(İç Kale)*, the highest point on the rock. The spot has sinister connections—it was once known as *adam atacağı* or "place from which man is thrown"—but the view across the shimmering Mediterranean, with a hint of turquoise in the blue, is truly magnificent.

That finger of rock you see advancing into the water is the **Cilvarda Burnu.** Three buildings hug it precariously: a defensive tower, a mint and—originally connected to the latter by stone steps—a monastery.

Boat trips visit an assortment of caves around the base of Alanya's immense rock. Hapless female victims of pirates were kept in the **Maidens' Cave**, on the east side; the **Lovers' Cave** needs no explanation. On the western side, the **Phosphorus Cave** glows with many hues; the much-visited **Damlataş** reputedly has the power to ease respira-

tory ailments. The stalactite and stalagmite formations resulting from the dripping of water over thousands of years, together with the humid heat, make it a soothing Turkish bath for local asthma sufferers.

Anamur

Just outside the town, down a lane overhung by trees, lie the ruins of **Anamuryum**, once a stylish Phoenician settlement embracing the southernmost point of Turkey's Mediterranean coast. Follow the trail through the arches and past storks nesting on higher parts to the pebble beach, where you can enjoy a quiet swim.

Larger than life, a huge rambling Byzantine fortress, **Mamure Kalesi**, grips the rock of the sea shore, 6 kilometres (4 mi.) east of Anamur. Its imposing ramparts are joined by 36

towers at strategic intervals. The castle was erected in the 3rd century and restored in 1230, and the Seljuks built a simple mosque in the grounds. The castle interior is gloomy—be careful if climbing to the battlements. Lizards dart over the cracked stone walls, and in the moat, fish and turtles provide a guaranteed distraction for children whose parents want to cool off in one of the open-air restaurants opposite.

Seljuk battlements crown Alanya; water carriers supply a precious commodity.

A few miles further on, past greenhouses bursting with banana palms, another ruined castle, the **Softa Kalesi,** dominates a high, craggy rock. The crumbling battlements command a good view but somehow look far less intimidating than the Mamure castle.

Silifke

In addition to the birds of passage that fly south to the sun, Silifke tempts an increasing number of holiday-makers. The tourists converge on the nearby beach of Taşucu on their way to northern Cyprus (2 hours by hovercraft, 6 by boat). The birds settle for the island of Dana, 60 seconds flight from Taşucu.

The town developed as an important commercial centre under the Romans, who built a bridge over the Göksu river. A thousand years later, German emperor Frederick Barbarossa crossed the river with the forces of the Third Crusade. He went back in for a swim and drowned.

Silifke's **castle** was built in Byzantine times and later furnished with a mosque by Sultan Beyazıt. Testimony to the benevolent climate, a giant **cistern,** 46 metres (151 ft.) long and half as wide, was carved out of the rocky hillside to store the town's precious supply of water.

Just outside Silifke, on the Antalya side, stand the remains of the **Basilica of St. Thecla** at Meryemlik. The basilica was built in the 5th century over the cave that Thecla, an early Christian martyr, occupied after following St. Paul through the mountains from Konya, where she had been converted by his teachings. A processional way was cut through the rock.

Some 20 kilometres (12 mi.) east of Silifke, in the village of **Narlıkuyu,** you can see the remains of Roman baths from the 4th century. A fine **mosaic floor** depicts the legendary Three Graces, and a nearby spring offers a variety of virtues—beauty, happiness, wisdom or wealth, with the bonus of a refreshing drink.

Asthma sufferers can try out a local remedy: the dank atmosphere of a cave just over a mile north is reputed to have a beneficial effect. The stalactites and stalagmites are eerie in torchlight. Be careful not to slip. Not far from here, you can descend into paradise at the **Heaven and Hell caves** *(Cennet ve Cehennem)*. It's quite easy to climb down into Heaven (a ruined Byzantine chapel stands at the entrance), but Hell is comfortingly inaccessible.

About 25 kilometres (15 mi.) from Silifke, further along the Mersin road, you reach **Kızkalesi,** once known as Corycos. A castle stands on the shore, another occupies a rock out at sea. According to legend, the king of ancient Corycos had the second castle built to keep his daughter safe after a soothsayer predicted she would die of a serpent bite. The princess was cosseted for years until the day she was sent a basket of grapes that contained a snake.

A valley of lemon trees leads to hundreds of rock tombs and other sarcophagi, and ruins of Byzantine churches.

Mersin and Tarsus

The sleek apartment blocks and hotels belie Mersin's impressive age: this bluff agricultural export town goes back well over 5,000 years. Mersin is a favourite embarkation point for boat trips to Cyprus and Syria. Much of the town's prosperity comes from agriculture and cotton, as it did in the 5th century B.C. Even then, Mersin had a respectable history—a hill 3 kilometres (2 mi.) inland, the Yümük Tepesi, has revealed a Neolithic settlement.

Tarsus lies about 28 kilometres (17 mi.) east of Mersin. It is the birthplace of St. Paul, who travelled around Asia Minor as the first Christian missionary. Tarsus is also the place where Mark Antony and Cleopatra met for the first time, in 41 B.C. They walked through **Cleopatra's Gate,** which had been erected in honour of the Egyptian queen. In those days, visitors could sail right into Tarsus; since then, the harbour has silted up and the sea has withdrawn. One of the more recent constructions, the **Great Mosque** *(Ulu Cami)* is representative of the 16th-century Ottoman style.

CENTRAL ANATOLIA

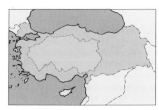

The dusty plateau begins at around 600 metres (1,968 ft.) above sea level and nudges its way between parched mountains, in places reaching almost twice the height. Wheat and barley are plentiful, and even in the mountains it's not all arid. An irregular strip of poplar trees frequently proclaims a river valley, a refreshing line of green among the stubble of the hillside. Every now and then a cluster of beehives appears, miles from habitation, owners camped close by to collect the honey for which central Anatolia is famed.

Ankara is the natural starting-point for a visit to central Anatolia. From there, Cappadocia, to the south-east, is a logical step. A good road from Nevşehir leads straight to Konya, itself only a few hours from the Mediterranean coast, taking in the prehistoric site of Çatalhüyük on the way. The ruins of Boğazköy-Hattuşaş, north-east of Ankara,

107

are easily accessible and have the added advantage of being on the direct route to the Black Sea coast.

ANKARA

Today's capital of Turkey is a far cry from the sad township that Kemal Atatürk visited in 1919. Then, many of the hastily built homes were made of mud, supplied by a stream which also brought the mosquitoes and malaria that plagued many of the 20,000 townspeople.

After 70 years, the transformation is total. Now Ankara is a boisterous city with well over 3 million inhabitants. Acacialined Atatürk Bulvarı, the main boulevard, cuts a broad swathe through the centre from north to south, setting the tone for an airy city so much less cramped—if less colourful—than Istanbul.

A two-day stay is the minimum needed for a relaxing tour of Ankara. If you're there for less, make sure you visit at least the Museum of Anatolian Civilizations (see p. 112), invaluable if you plan to see the ancient cities of the region.

The Old Town

Most of the sights of Ankara are grouped together in the same section of town, north of Talatpaşa Bulvarı. Start out from **Ulus Meydanı** (Nation Square), where you'll see a statue of Atatürk on

horseback. The statue also illustrates the role of the woman in modern Turkey. She is shown in the background behind two armed soldiers, carrying a shell for the independence struggle.

Just off the square, the **Column of Julian** *(Julianus Sütunu)* provides a handy pedestal for the resident stork. The column was erected to commemorate a visit made by the Roman emperor in 362.

The **Mosque of Hacı Bayram** *(Hacı Bayram Camii)*, close by, contains the sarcophagi of the founder of the 15th-century mosque and members of his family. Next door are the remains of the **Temple of Augustus** *(Augustus Mabedi)*, now inhabited by pigeons. A succession of places of worship occupied the site, each handed on and converted, from Phrygians to Romans to Byzantines to Seljuk Turks. Try reading the inscriptions detailing the achievements of the Roman emperor Augustus. From here, you can see across to the north wall of Ankara's citadel, the fortifications embedded firmly in the rough rock and surrounded by scrub.

Cross Çankırı Caddesi, a continuation of Atatürk Bulvarı, to the ruins of the **Roman Baths** *(Roma Hamamı)*. Neatly blending modern brick walls frame the original bath area which contained a pool, changing cubicles and full central heating 3rd-century style. Note the myriad tiny holes in the underground system, and watch your step—the ground is full of dangerous gaps.

A rabbit-warren of houses, many of them defying the laws of gravity, surrounds the oldest part of Ankara, the **Citadel** *(Hisar)*. A taxi can get you there, weaving skilfully past baskets of spice, pots and pans and urchins dodging across the narrow streets. From the terrace, you can look down on the green and pleasant pastures of the modern city. The sweeping view shows the mausoleum of Atatürk across on a hill to the south-west, then the lake and fountain of Gençlik Park with, beyond it, the racecourse. Next come the Roman ruins and mosque of Hacı Bayram, the limits of the city 70 years ago.

Around to the right is Hıdırlık Hill, one of Ankara's poorest areas that nonetheless manages to vibrate with colour. The ant-hill of homes is known as the Golden Mountain, although the shanty-town houses are predominantly deep turquoise, interspersed with the green of beeches and acacias.

In 1290 the Seljuks built the **Mosque of the Lion House** *(Arslanhane Camii)*, south of the Citadel. As you enter by the upper courtyard, which doubles as a local football pitch, you'll feel a sudden dip in the temperature. You'll also notice the 3-foot-high steel safe, designed to encourage the most reticent of donors. A wicker fence conceals women worshippers from the eyes of the men below. The obvious white stone chapters at the top of the 24 columns tell you they came from the Roman ruins, but the columns themselves have been painted an unhappy wood-brown in an attempt to match the pine above. Downstairs, you can better view the impressive staircase and platform of the carved *mimber* from which the imam gives his Friday address. Five varnished wooden clocks remind the faithful of the times of daily prayer, each fixed to the minute with the remorseless precision of a Swiss watch. A sixth shows the time for fasting.

Modern Ankara

By virtue of its splendid setting, the **Atatürk Mausoleum** *(Anıt Kabir)* stands head and shoulders above anything else in Ankara. The long walk to the mausoleum itself is guarded by stone lions and giant statues of men denoting education, agriculture and the armed forces—three pillars in Atatürk's conception of the state. Equalling them in stature: three women. Inside, the sarcophagus rests on a marble floor. The roof is supported by huge limestone columns.

Quotations from Atatürk's speeches are inscribed in gold. Another inscription in the entrance to the adjoining **Museum** *(Müze)* expresses his long-cherished ideal of a Turkish republic with independence and no outside interference. His two identity cards are displayed—the original one in Arabic, issued after his birth in Thessalonika (''Selânik''), the second in Roman letters after he revolutionized the alphabet. A symbolic gold key is there, presented to Atatürk by the people of Samsun to commemorate his landing in 1919 (see p. 129).

Many people come simply for a look at the personal belongings, to try to get closer to a man revered throughout Turkey to this day. There is likely to be a crowd of people around a black-and-white photograph taken during a ceremony marking the tenth anniversary of his death. Look beyond the army officer to the cloud in the sky. It bears a striking resemblance to Atatürk's profile.

If you're in Ankara on a Sunday afternoon, take a taxi to the **President's House** *(Atatürk Köşkü),* high up in Ankara's fashionable southern district of

Of breathtaking beauty, words from the Koran in the Museum of Ethnography.

Çankaya (it's closed to the public the rest of the week). Atatürk spent the early years of his presidency here. The avenue that curves round to the house is flanked by imposing beeches; the grounds are tastefully landscaped around an ornamental pond. The *köşk* is unmistakably Atatürk, with the same corner tower (added after he moved in) as his summer house in Trabzon (see p. 134). Whereas the official rooms reflect the pomp of state ceremony, the private rooms mirror the Turkish leader's personal economy and simplicity of style. Presidential mansion or not, Atatürk would allow people to call it only ''The president's home''.

The house was presented to him in 1921 by the mufti, the religious leader of the comparatively insignificant township of Ankara. For the following 11 years he lived there, formulating—then implementing—the structure and policy of his republic. A framed portrait shows one of the people who most influenced his thinking, particularly over the status of women: his mother, Zübeyde Hanım. Among the elegant trappings, the house had central heating, a status symbol indeed in those days. Unfortunately, it rarely worked, but the problem was partly solved by the use of a brass brazier, still there today, that could be filled with hot coals or wood.

A fitting climax to any day of sightseeing is undoubtedly the **Kocatepe Camii,** a magnificently successful exercise in blending Ottoman grandeur and modern style. Its stunning lighting is best seen at night. Don't be deterred by an air of unreadiness outside—the mosque has been under construction for 30 years and still has one or two to go.

The central dome unfolds from the others like a flower in full bloom, framed by four magnificent minarets. Inside, an enormous chandelier is suspended in the shape of a sun, the crystal reflecting all the colours of the spectrum. Thirty-two miniature chandeliers, also ball-shaped, daintily complement it.

Walk across the hall to see the grace of the main dome, surrounded by four corner domes and twelve smaller outer ones, each traced with fine pastel patterns. Matching the effect, in colour if not value, are the dozens of brightly coloured glass prayer bead sets scattered around, each *tespih* on loan for spontaneous thanksgiving.

Beneath the mosque floor, back down to earth: a giant car park was one of the most important features of planning, to accommodate the thousands of Turks who come to see the Kocatepe.

The Museums

Not far from Opera Meydanı, the **Museum of Ethnography** *(Etnografya Müzesi)* has the last word in Ottoman fashions, with a dazzling array of minutely worked embroidery and other forms of needlework. The collection of carpets and kilims is fascinating; each piece tells its own tale, woven with themes of love, jealousy, hope and happiness.

The metalwork section covers a wide range from the 11th century to the 19th, including a picnic box, a soap dish for the public baths, a healing bowl and a *şerbet kazanı,* a kettle that was used to serve fruit juice to guests. The Ottoman glassware and porcelain dishes are finely decorated with delicate flower motifs, a form which developed in view of the Islamic ban on pictorial representation of the human form.

An easy walk from the Citadel, the **Museum of Anatolian Civilizations** *(Anadolu Medeniyetleri Müzesi)* is a treasure trove of finds, mainly from the Hittite Period. Exhibits are contained in a restored *bedesten,* a covered bazaar built in the 15th century by the grand vizier of Mehmet the Conqueror. The

Eyes that have seen 3,000 years pass by: a sacred Hittite bull in the Museum of Anatolian Civilizations.

museum is organized in chronological order, with a hall devoted to Hittite sculpture down the middle.

A huge limestone **Hittite king** greets you as you enter. He was unearthed at the palace of Arslantepe, near Malatya, where, since the 8th century B.C., he had been toasting his warriors' victory over the Assyrians.

Neolithic man's early religious beliefs can be seen in the hunting and dancing scenes of **friezes** found at Çatalhüyük, near Konya (see p. 128). The red and black matchstick figures were painted with a surprisingly accurate sense of movement and proportion, considering they are from the dawn of civilization.

A set of 11 **figurines** represents the trials of primitive woman. Different poses lead from virgin, through pregnancy to childbirth and motherhood. Also from Çatalhüyük, a sun-dried clay figure of a goddess, giving birth, with a sacred leopard on either side as her baby emerges looks rather like a plump woman in an armchair.

One of the most interesting Bronze Age items is a stag flanked by two bulls in a round, twisted frame representing the sun, with an antler-shaped base. Such sculptures were left in Hatti royal tombs to facilitate reincarnation of the occupants as gods or goddesses. You may have noticed the trio itself reborn in splendid style as a huge bronze statue on Atatürk Bulvarı.

Don't miss the delightful **children's toys.** Even in 2500 B.C., there was an imaginative assortment of clay animals, not to mention the miniature pitchers containing tiny stones—baby's first rattle.

The large **tablets** covered in cuneiform script, complete with clay "envelopes", are examples of business contracts agreed by the Assyrian traders who settled outside the cities in early Hittite times. Note the double-headed eagle that appears on the sophisticated stamps and seals developed by the Hittites.

Other exhibits include coins from the Lydian Period in gold, silver and electrum—a natural alloy of the two precious metals. And as you complete your tour, don't miss the rare bottle of perfume, treasured by a Roman woman some 1,800 years ago. The pale green liquid and glass container with delicate flower pattern have survived intact since the 2nd century.

Boğazköy-Hattuşaş

The 200-kilometre (127-mi.) journey to the former centre of the Hittite kingdom can be covered by bus as far as Sungurlu, and from there by taxi to the village of Boğazkale. Heading east out of Ankara, you see the

Koroğlu mountains rising in the distance. Closer to Sungurlu, irrigated green grass and ochre hillsides stand out starkly against the blue sky. The turning, to the right, is just beyond Sungurlu.

The simple stone building of the Boğazköy Museum is partly concealed by a row of poplar trees at the entrance to the village. It contains some less important finds from the German excavations that began in 1906 and resumed after World War II.

Beyond the dry-stone houses of Boğazkale, rugged rocks on the hillside divert your attention from the sprawl of stones to the right. This is the start of **Boğazköy,** the area which comprises Hattuşaş and Yazılıkaya. Follow the path round to the sign "Büyükmabet" (Great Temple). Here you see storehouses and clay jars—the biggest of which held almost 3,000 litres—but little else. The temple, a single-storey, flat-roofed building, is thought to have been dedicated to the storm god and the sun goddess.

The mass of stone is confusing. The best way to orient yourself is to continue up the track to the **Great Fortress** *(Büyükkale),* royal residence of ancient Hattuşaş.

Climb the rough-hewn steps (the Hittites used a ramp) for a magnificent view across the verdant plain towards the Black Sea. Below, the temple layout is suddenly clear.

In Büyükkale, the upper and middle buildings formed part of the king's residence, with linking courtyards and fine houses for nobles. The complex was destroyed around 1200 B.C., partly by a disastrous fire. Blackened rocks are still in evidence. One floor caved in on another, burying tablets that comprised practically the whole recorded history of the Hittite civilization. They remained untouched for 3,000 years. Then, in 1906, about 2,500 texts were discovered, among them the peace treaty between King Hattusilis III and the Egyptian pharaoh Ramses II, who married one of the Hittite king's daughters, thus cementing relations between the two empires. Another 3,000 pieces of tablet were found almost 30 years later, and a statue of Cybele, the Phrygian fertility goddess, was also uncovered.

The path continues round to the **Royal Gate** *(Kralkapısı),* so called because the relief of the war god found there was mistaken for a king. His left hand is raised to protect the gate and those who walk through it. This is just a copy of the original, now in Ankara's Museum of Anatolian Civilizations. It's not the only imitation to be found at Boğazköy—many local youngsters do a brisk trade in reliefs and tablets with unsuspecting tourists. Whatever you are offered, if it's genuine it's against the law and if not, it's a waste of money.

Next gate is the **Yerkapı**, a triangular-shaped underground passage, dank and chill, cutting 71 metres (233 ft.) through the city ramparts. Two limestone sphinxes guarded the postern gate. And as a practical aid to keeping out unwanted visitors,

the slope outside the city was paved, therefore slippery.

The circular route takes you on around the old city walls to the **Lion Gate** *(Aslanlıkapı)*. Walk through to see the once-fierce pair. One of them is toothless and tired-looking, the other has lost most of its head.

It takes 5 minutes by taxi from Boğazkale to reach the rock sanctuary of **Yazılıkaya**, thought to

have been built by King Tudhaliya IV, who features prominently in the reliefs there. Walking through the main chamber, you are greeted by a frieze of 12 gods. The general rule is, with a few exceptions, gods on the left, goddesses on the right. One particularly imposing scene shows the storm god Teshub and his wife Hepatu, sun goddess, celebrating the advent of spring with a cup of something appropriate. A panther, a double-headed eagle, mountains and mere mortals surround them. In the main relief, King Tudhaliya walks on the mountaintops.

A narrow crevice leads through to the smaller rock chamber. Look carefully for the two guards, half-man, half-lion, barely perceptible on each side of the entrance. Twelve more gods line up for the cameras and King Tudhaliya appears again, protected by the Sun God.

The clearing is a perfect setting for a sanctuary. A constant chattering from high up in the rocks shows that birds also find it one. The site is kept unusually tidy, thanks to the post-Hittite blue rubbish bin that appeals: Şehrimize temiz tutalım (Keep our city clean).

CAPPADOCIA

Comparisons range from fairy chimneys and moonscapes to fossilized mushrooms and much ruder. The descriptions may differ but the conclusion is the same: it's a wonder of nature, unequalled anywhere else in the world.

The secret of Cappadocia is its tuff, a rock formed by volcanic ash millions of years ago. Boul-

Carved out of the rock by wind and rain—unearthly Cappadocia.

ders of hard rock sheltered the tuff immediately below from the wind and rain, which ate away the rest. As a result, tall columns capped with rocks gradually appeared. When, 1,400 years ago, Arab armies invaded the region, the Christian inhabitants found they could tunnel into the porous rock and fashion homes overnight. Whenever the Arabs came, the Christians went underground, establishing at one time ten cities and almost 400 churches and chapels.

Cappadocia consists of three ravaged valleys—Göreme, Soğanlı and Ihlara. Each of them can be covered in one day. Although Göreme and Ürgüp are popular centres, many people prefer to base themselves in Nevşehir, which itself has other historical sights.

Nevşehir

From below, the recently restored crenellations on the **Fortress** *(Kale)* stand out pale against the basalt rock, humped into place when Nevşehir became a stopping point on the Silk Route in the 13th century. You can look down from the battlements on the sandstone minarets of some of the city's 52 mosques —a symphony of sound echoes through the city when the muezzin begin their calls to prayer. You feel a sense of isolation until you glance across at the spread of apartment blocks, built to accommodate Nevşehir's population which has doubled in 20 years.

Since the **Kurşunlu Camii** was constructed in 1727, some of its turquoise ceramic stars have fallen, but the mosque remains a fitting centrepiece of the Ottoman complex—library, kitchens, caravanserai, baths and *medrese* for theological studies.

Eight stone pillars take the weight of the dome. Competing for size are the immense candles, tilting in their copper stands towards Mecca on either side of the *mihrab*. The mosque's flower designs add warmth to the stone with a colourful blend of red, blue and brown.

Nevşehir's **Museum** *(Müze)*, opened in 1987, has a collection of objects from the 3rd millennium B.C. to the late Ottoman period, all found in the province. Three Roman tombs lie side by side, unknown skulls added rather unnecessarily, to show which way round the bodies are. There are terracotta Phrygian utensils, pretty mother-of-pearl Byzantine jewellery and even Roman tear glasses from the 3rd century, used for collecting the woman's tears when her loved one died.

All over Anatolia,
girls in flowered pantaloons
lend a helping hand.

Göreme Valley

On the road east of Nevşehir, **Uçhisar** stands out against the skyline, a rock castle seemingly split in two. Surrounded by rocks resembling petrified monks' cowls, the castle takes on the aspect of a grotesque many-faced theatre mask. Geyser-like bursts of sandstone are everywhere, riddled with homes tailormade for the troglodyte, pockmarked with holes that serve as windows.

The village of **Göreme** has melted into its surroundings, modern restaurants carved into the soft stone. The style becomes so natural that the minaret of a mosque looks suddenly out of place in this sci-fi setting. Göreme's extensive open-air museum has a convent on the left and monastery on the right. The two were not connected, no matter what any guide may tell you.

The misshapen rocks belie the beauty of the churches carved inside them. Frescoes are in two stages, the earliest dating mainly from the 8th century and devoted to the life of Christ. Often they deteriorate towards ground level, where the plaster was easy picking for early souvenir hunters. One of the finest examples of rock-church frescoes is the **Apple Church** *(Elmalı Kilise)*.

As you head north for the village of Zelve, the tortured tuff flattens into two dimensions.

Then you are confronted by mushroom formations at the **Pasha's Vineyard** *(Paşabağı)*, so called because of the rich sandy soil found to be nutritious for grapes, as well as potatoes and other vegetables. Beyond the apricot trees, the towers retain their hard summits, while the rest is eroded by centuries of wind. **Zelve**—a ghost town since 1950—is now an open-air museum.

The workshops of **Avanos** are noted for their prolific potters. All manner of souvenirs, including objects of alabaster and onyx, are fashioned here. The Kızılırmak (Red River), which flows through town, provides red clay for the local earthenware.

Take the easternmost road from here to Ürgüp to see the **Valley of Fairy Chimneys** *(Peribacalar Vadisi)*, where hundreds of these strange formations cluster together.

Soğanlı Valley

You can reach this valley via Ürgüp, or make a long round trip taking in the underground cities of Kaymaklı and Derinkuyu, south of Nevşehir.

The villagers of **Kaymaklı** lived a double life. Normal homes were built on the neighbouring hill, known as Göztepe (Lookout Hill), where guards would warn of any invasion.

In Göreme's Yılanlı Church, Sts. George and Theodore, local heroes, slay the fearsome dragon.

Whenever danger threatened, the villagers would descend by tunnel to underground sanctuaries scooped out around a 65-metre (213-ft.) central pillar.

Tour coaches converge on the car park, and their occupants file in just as the inhabitants of Kaymaklı did, but with the aid of electric lighting. Of the eight floors, the one at ground level, thought to have been a hospital, and the bottom three are blocked. You descend to the first underground level, where animals were kept and fed, and then to the others—most of the time bent double. The maze of passages leads through living quarters to a tiny Byzantine church, crude crosses faintly scratched on the wall.

121

One inconvenience of life underground was disposal of the dead. The people of Kaymaklı met this problem in the same way that Neolithic man did 7,000 years earlier: the deceased were buried in the floor of the home, rocks covering the bodies. Grids today show some of the dining-room graves. You can also see the circular granite doors that were rolled shut whenever the subterranean city was attacked. Anyone who did make it into the passages would still be un-prepared for the hidden forms of defence—other parts of the tun-nel were blocked off and the attackers themselves attacked, unseen, through knee-level holes in the walls. One door doubled as a spice-crushing table when the coast was clear.

Halfway down, note the dual-purpose shaft that provided water from the well at the bottom and fresh air from the top for all connecting levels. The kitchens were blackened by smoke from constant use, even though chimneys dispersed the smoke, releasing it well away from any entrance. Wine-making crevices were also dug, a channel taking out the wine pressed from the grapes by foot.

The city of **Derinkuyu**, 9 kilo-

Dramatic shadows make the fairy chimneys all the more intriguing.

metres (5 mi.) further south, descends eight levels to three times the depth of Kaymaklı. A tunnel joined the two cities, but it has not been excavated.

Nowadays, pigeons outnumber human visitors to the Soğanlı Valley. Flat-topped mountains rise up high above the pinnacle rocks containing churches, monasteries—and dovecots, painted white to signal the way for errant birds. Their droppings are collected by villagers for use as fertilizer. Of the valley's many churches and monasteries, the **Karabaş** is noted for its frescoes, particularly one depicting the communion of the Twelve Apostles.

Ihlara Valley

Up to 100,000 people once inhabited this dramatic, twisting canyon, 45 kilometres (28 mi.) south-east of Aksaray. A winding line of trees reveals the refreshing presence of a stream down at the bottom.

More than 105 Byzantine churches were built or cut into the rock in the 15-kilometre (9-mi.) valley. The **Ağaçaltı** or Daniel church has comparatively well-preserved frescoes, notably one of Daniel with the lions. Themes in the **Yılanlı** (Snake) church include St. Michael weighing good and evil in a balance and serpents entwining the wicked.

KONYA

An atmosphere of cheerful pandemonium reigns in Turkey's oldest city. Horse-drawn vehicles of every kind trundle through the old town centre, prompting the appearance of the first "No carts allowed" signs. The buildings may be new, but habits are old. As many centuries as miles separate Konya from the Mediterranean resort towns.

St. Paul preached in Konya with Barnabas, but had to flee the city when members of the Jewish population plotted against them. Twelve hundred years later, the mystic philosopher Celaleddin Rumi, known as Mevlana (Our Master), met a more receptive audience when he founded a sect that became known as the Whirling Dervishes.

Seljuk sultan Alaettin Keykubat left his stamp on the town with a number of impressive edifices, but Konya is mainly Mevlana, and the first place to visit is the **Mevlana Müzesi,** his museum and mausoleum. Souvenir shops have Mevlana mementos and you can even arrive in style in a Mevlana taxi. But the moment you enter the building, the superficiality comes to an abrupt end. The awed hush is one rarely found in the greatest of mosques. In the background, a *ney*—the reed instrument that traditionally plays Mevlana's music—pipes a continuous wailing lament.

Mevlana's **tomb**—directly underneath the conical Green Dome—has a green brocade cover embroidered with gold thread. Next to the sarcophagus is that of his first son, Sultan Veled. The other 65 coffins bear the bodies of Mevlana's followers and relatives from 1273, when he died. The **Silver Cage and**

All You Need is Love

Mevlana came to Konya from Persia in 1228. Following in his father's footsteps, he became a sufi, *a mystical theologian, teaching in one of Konya's religious schools*.

The turning point in Mevlana's career was a chance meeting with a wandering dervish, Shams, in 1244. Mevlana was captivated by the personality of this man, in whom he found the ultimate expression of divine perfection. For months the two mystics lived closely together, scandalizing Mevlana's neglected family and disciples. The close relationship was too much to take, and eventually Shams was quietly disposed of— not without a little help from Mevlana's sons.

The distress that Mevlana felt at the loss of his loved one turned him into a prolific poet, composing most of his verses in a state of music-induced ecstasy.

One day, a few years after the death of Shams, Mevlana was attracted by the sound of a goldsmith hammering in front of his shop, and he began a whirling dance to the sound of the hammer. His friendship with the goldsmith,

Salahaddin, again inspired him to write poetry. Salahaddin died and was replaced in Mevlana's affections by Chelebi Husameddin, who followed him around noting down his verses as he composed them— even in the bath.

After his death, Mevlana's fraternity of disciples was organized into a group called the Mevlevi sect, known in the West as the Whirling Dervishes. Their dancing ceremony, or sama, is a way of communicating with God. Whirling faster and faster, they enter a state of trance, attempting to lose their personal identities to attain complete union with the Almighty. The Mevlevi student has a tough initiation, described as the "Thousand and One Days of Penitence". Learning to whirl starts with a bruising foot-balancing exercise, wrapping two toes round a nail and turning on the spot.

Though the sufi *brotherhoods were dissolved by governmental decree in 1925, special permission was granted the Mevlevi dervishes in 1954 to perform their ritual dances two weeks every year, in December.*

125

Threshold herald the entrance to the burial chamber.

Some idea of the mystic's standing can be gleaned from the **April Bowl**, a bronze urn patterned in gold and silver. It was used to collect rain water that fell during April and, according to Islamic belief, was both sacred and beneficial for some ailments. The healing water doubled its powers when Mevlana's turban touched it.

Note the two giant sets of prayer beads hanging up, each *tespih* containing 990 beads of walnut and lime. Also on show are the Beard of the Prophet, Mevlana's prayer mat, and priceless manuscripts including copies of the Koran from Seljuk and Ottoman times and Mevlana's most famous work, the Masnawi—six volumes consisting of 25,618 couplets.

The **Koyunoğlu Museum and Library** (*A.R. İzzet Koyunoğlu Şehir Müzesi ve Kütüphanesi*) has sections devoted to Seljuk and Ottoman embroidery and handicrafts as well as carpets, prayer mats and examples of the *cicim,* a thicker version of the kilim. In another section you can see primitive tools in obsidian from the Palaeolithic and Neolithic ages and Early Bronze age vessels. Some of the finds are from nearby Çatalhüyük.

In the centre of town, beside the remains of a Seljuk palace,

stands the **Alaettin Camii**, the mosque named after Konya's second most famous personality, Sultan Keykubat, and built during his reign in 1221. Of particular interest are the excellent carved wooden *mihrab* and *mimber*. The stone pillars, with the weight of centuries upon them, have been relieved by supporting beams.

A sea of restful blue awaits

you in the nearby **Karatay Mü-zesi,** the ceramics museum installed in a domed *medrese* built for religious studies in 1251. The marble portal is intricately patterned, but the interior, once entirely covered with tiles, is now incomplete.

The plain stone bath in the centre of the hall was not meant for dangling the feet in but for the more esoteric study of astronomy. Star-gazing students would lean over the edge, holding their breath in order not to cause ripples, and plot the heavenly bodies reflected through the opening in the domed roof.

The **Slender Minaret Museum** *(İnce Minare Müzesi)* was also

Improvised transport in Konya,
a lively town
isolated in a barren steppe.

designed in the 13th century as a theological school. Nowadays, the minaret is not so much *ince* as *kisa* (short)—the result of a wayward flash of lightning. But the magnificent Seljuk Baroque portal escaped damage. Turquoise-blue tiles shine in the stone like jewels. The building was converted into a museum this century; its lead dome shelters tombstone carvings and headstones found in the area. Note the recurring Seljuk emblem, the two-headed eagle.

Pride of place at the **Museum of Archaeology** *(Arkeoloji Müzesi)* goes to the Roman tomb with a splendidly detailed basrelief depicting Hercules making light work of his 12 tasks. More sarcophagi and accessories were found during excavations at Çatalhüyük and other sites.

Çatalhüyük

A visit to this ancient site, 60 kilometres (37 mi.) south-east of Konya, may not yield any archaeological marvels but is good for the soul—it is fascinating simply to stand on the spot where Stone Age man established one of the very first human settlements more than 9,000 years ago.

Çatalhüyük is reached via the Karaman road from Konya. Turn off at Çumra. The road leads across an ancient railway line, past ungainly concrete electricity poles to a dirt road bordered by fields of wheat and sugar beet. At the T-junction, turn left. A sign further on directs you to the right and a small stone cottage.

The elderly guardian shades you ceremonially from the sun with an umbrella and gives a halting and unstoppable litany in any one of several languages acquired over the past 20 years.

Not much remains of the settlement, apart from humps and depressions in an open field, although you can spot flakes of bone in the earth as well as fragments of obsidian and pieces of stone that were shaped into balllike weapons.

The ancient community was made up of 2,000 square mudblock homes, each sheltering a family of four to five people. There were no windows or doors—access was by a hole in the roof which also served as ventilation shaft and chimney.

In one of the depressions was a temple containing bulls' horns and friezes now in the Museum of Anatolian Civilizations in Ankara. Of the two main settlements *(hüyük)*, covering 14 hectares (34 acres) of hillside, only one has been excavated. Twelve levels were revealed, from the Palaeolithic, Neolithic, Chalcolithic and Mesolithic periods. Further digs are expected to bring important discoveries.

BLACK SEA COAST

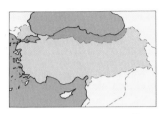

From the tobacco fields of Sinop to the cornfields and hazelnut plantations of Samsun, the cherry trees of Giresun and the acres of tea at Rize, Turkey's northernmost provinces make up a pretty patchwork of colour.

The coast stretches 1,695 kilometres (1,053 mi.) from Bulgaria to the Soviet frontier. The most attractive region, apart from the beaches close to the Bosphorus, lies between Samsun and Trabzon—old Trebizond.

The northern coast is slightly remote; few roads cut through the mountain range. But as the ancient kingdom of Pontus, it was more than happy with a certain isolation. Nowadays, the people are just as warm and welcoming as the rest of the Turks, simply more shy.

Towards the east the rain is less predictable and the Georgian accent more pronounced, as the Kaçkar mountains fold round to the Russian border.

Samsun to Tirebolu

Samsun has been a commercial port since Milesian colonists realized its potential as far back as the 7th century B.C. The bracing air and overwhelming friendliness of the people more than make up for the functional railway siding that cordons off the sea front. And Samsun has a special place in every Turk's heart: this is the City of 19th May, where Atatürk arrived at the start of his struggle for a republic.

It is difficult to miss Samsun's most striking mosque, the **Merkez Cami,** also known as the Yeni Cami (New Mosque) as it was completed only in 1982. The marble minaret points 48 metres (157 ft.) like a space rocket ready for take-off. Equally impressive is the metal-plated dome reflecting the sun like a giant armadillo. Once on the green and red striped carpeting you will be struck by the simplicity of the stained-glass windows and dome, the latter stained by leaking rain water. On either side of the central *mihrab*, a grandfather clock stands sentinel. Steps at the side of the entrance lead down into the modern shopping arcade underneath the mosque.

Centrepiece of the **Museum of Ethnography** *(Etnografya Müzesi)* is a reassembled mosaic floor some 10 metres (33 ft.) square, depicting the four seasons and tales from Roman mythology. Commissioned during the reign of Emperor Severus Alexander, it was found worthy of repair when the city became a Byzantine province. You can make out one of the unending battles at sea between the Nereids, or nymphs, and Tritons.

Next door, the **Atatürk Museum** *(Atatürk Müzesi)* contains personal effects and framed sheaves of tobacco presented to Atatürk after his arrival in 1919.

At the edge of Atatürk Bulvarı, the **"First Step" monument** marks the Turkish leader's landing in Samsun. Further along, on the other side, is an acclaimed statue of Atatürk mounted and in action.

For one of the best views out over the harbour and the Black Sea, head for the hill on the out-

skirts of the city past an army base, to Samsun's airport. It was built recently for small aircraft, known to local people as "pır-pırs" because of their engine noise.

Once through the untidy outskirts of Samsun, the road ventures briefly inland. The Canik mountains emerge beyond the village of Terme, subsiding as you near **Ünye**, 89 kilometres

(56 mi.) from Samsun and worth a lunchtime stop for its fish. The seaport appears around a corner, set snugly in a pretty bay. Pine trees shelter nearby Çamlık beach.

The fishing port of **Ordu**, 79 kilometres (48 mi.) east of Ünye,

*Threading tobacco leaves
while baby sleeps; and Trabzon's
St. Sophia.*

also has a tempting beach, Güzelyalı, a mile beyond it. This was the most welcome sight in the world for survivors of a force of 10,000 Greek mercenaries in 401 B.C. They had marched without food all the way from Mesopotamia after being defeated in battle.

Beyond Piraziz—whose friendly "Well Come" and "Bye Bye" merit at least a stop for tea—are more beaches, and a series of conical forested hills inland.

The town of cherry fame, **Giresun**, straddles a hilly promontory 50 kilometres (31 mi.) from Ordu, its Byzantine fortress commanding a good view over the placid Black Sea. The first cherry trees introduced to Italy came from here; the town's original name, Cerasos, gave its name to cherries in many European languages. On a nearby island, **Giresun Adası**, you can see the remains of a temple dedicated to Ares, the god of war (the Romans called him Mars).

A worsening road leads through a sharp cleft in the mountain and into succulent green valleys. Other beaches follow, then the ruins of the medieval castle of **Tirebolu**, contrasting with the tree-lined main street of today's trim fishing village.

A sandy beach appears, and the mountains inland give way to the Harşit stream. Beyond it,

white beach, sand and pebbles stretch as far as the eye can see. Thirty kilometres (19 mi.) from Trabzon, the road deteriorates further. You may think you're seeing double, with two villages called Mersin (Myrtle), northeastern counterparts of the Mediterranean resort.

Trabzon

Many Turks come to explore this fascinating city, which sprawls grandiosely on either side of a gorge giving splendid views of the old fortifications and harbour. Because of the city's rambling design, much of which looks unplanned, finding your way around takes time. A *dolmuş* or taxi tour is the best solution. As always, the tourist office should be the first port of call.

Trabzon's oldest church, **Küçük Ayvasıl Kilisesi** (St. Ann's) is conveniently located opposite the post office, but it is still easy to miss. Weeds on the roof relieve the grey stone of the building, constructed in the 7th century and restored around 200 years later by Emperor Basil I. Subsequently, the church was used for burials (it is the only one in Trabzon built above a crypt) and coffins remained there until just over a hundred years ago.

West of the city, set high up in rose gardens overlooking the sea, is the **St. Sophia Museum** *(Aya-*

sofya Müzesi), a unique achievement in Byzantine architecture. It was the dream of the Emperor of Trebizond, Manuel I, to create something that would bear comparison with the great Ayasofya mosque in Constantinople. He put a lot of energy—and money—into a monastery that contained the church of St. Sophia, now the museum.

The three large barrel-vaulted porches and a podium to raise the building above the ground were a first step—nothing like it was known in Byzantine church design. Then Manuel ordered artists to lavishly decorate the church. A mixture of Byzantine and Seljuk style resulted, since those working on it included Seljuks fleeing from the Mongols. The costliest pigments—including ultramarine blue—were used for biblical scenes on the dome, narthex and porches. Christ is shown on the dome, the Apostles on the drum between the windows, and the Prophets within. Angels in adoration on a frieze complete the picture.

The exterior of the south porch carries the downfall of Adam and Eve in relief, from the forbidden fruit to their expulsion from Paradise. Despite erosion of the stone figures, there is a definite hint of repentance in their pose. The final scene shows the resulting offspring, Cain, killing his brother, Abel. The work of early graffiti artists can be seen on the exterior of the apses, pictures of sailing ships thought to have been surreptitious requests for safe conduct at the start of a sea voyage.

The **Ortahisar** or Fatih Büyük Camii, the mosque in the Citadel, began life as a Byzantine church dedicated to St. Andrew. When the city became a metropolitan seat in the 8th century, the church was elevated to cathedral status and for an unknown reason changed its allegiance to the Virgin of the Golden Head (Panaghia Chrysokephalos).

When Sultan Mehmet II took over the city in 1461, a change of faith was in order. The south porch was added and, most important, the *mihrab* was installed on the new mosque where the centre of the church's south balcony had been. Today, the bright red and green carpets with a recurring *mihrab* design point the way for prayer.

The Byzantine city walls and ruins of the **Fortress** *(Kale)* rise majestically on the trapezoidshaped ledge which gave the city its early name, Trapezus. The view down over the gorge that splits the city is worth the walk. The walls of the lower city were put up by Hadrian and rebuilt by the Ottomans. Trabzon's great divide became less pronounced

Miraculously embedded in the mountainside, Sumela Monastery.

when the Turks took over. They demolished the drawbridges that isolated the fortress and joined the two sides with viaducts.

The **Gülbahar Hatun Camii** was the first Ottoman mosque in Trabzon, built in 1491 for Mehmet the Conqueror's daughter-in-law (and Suleiman the Magnificent's grandmother) Princess Ayşe Hatun. The name Gülbahar (Spring Rose) was given to Ayşe because of her great popularity with the people.

Up in the hills outside Trabzon, set among spruce trees, is the villa where Atatürk once stayed, the **Atatürk Köşkü**. Three nights were long enough for him to fall in love with the wedding-cake design and for the city to present him with the villa. The finely chiselled white stone stands out brightly, enveloped for much of the year in a scent of roses. Inside, Atatürk's straightforward living style contrasts with the extravagant architecture. Work on the house began at the end of the last century, with materials brought from Russia. One downstairs room has a special significance: it was here that Atatürk signed his will, leaving everything to the Turkish people.

Sumela Monastery

A vision 1,600 years ago led to the building of one of the most fascinating sights in north-eastern Turkey: the Sumela Monastery (Meryemana on some maps). It was the work of two Athenian priests, who trekked some 47 kilometres (30 mi.) south-west of Trabzon in search of the appointed place. It turned out to be a test for a true masochist—small caves hundreds of

feet up in the rock that were just about accessible to a healthy mountain goat. The two priests established a monastery that was to become respected throughout the kingdom of Pontus.

In the 6th century, the Emperor Justinian saw the strategic possibilities of the monastery and, as well as donating valuable items, strengthened the buildings. His measures didn't deter roving bands of robbers, though, and the place was cleaned out. Subsequent Byzantine emperors took an interest in Sumela. In return for coronation in the small Church of the Assumption, they restored, added to and enriched the monastery. They also left their signatures, in the form of flattering frescoes.

You can reach Sumela via the town of Maçka, turning off through a picturesque valley that becomes more enchanting as the road becomes more appalling. Through the dust, a towering mountain looms up. The monastery clings to the sheer rock face. Even 20th-century transport only postpones the inevitable: today's clamber is every bit as punishing as it was in the 4th century. But it's worth it. Allow a good half hour and check first that the monastery is open for viewing (normally 9 a.m.–5 p.m.). An umbrella is a useful accessory—mist and cloud are often encountered this high above the rushing Meksila river, and it frequently rains.

If the guard is in the alcove of his hut, wait a moment—he will be praying. Outside the monastery, the **Sacred Spring** *(Ayazma)* has been dripping steadily for thousands of years from a rock overhang 40 metres (131 ft.) up, attracting prayers and hopes. More recent low-denomination coins help reinforce the requests.

Inside, the original church frescoes from the 9th century are exposed in parts by the flaking of the later layer of frescoes from Ottoman times. Throughout, holes appear in the walls, and much of the plaster has gone. The wardens put it all down to "American tourists". Spot the discreetly chalked "1741", a reminder to forgetful guides of the date of the later frescoes. It goes unnoticed in the jungle of graffiti.

EASTERN TURKEY

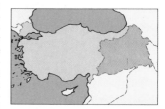

It may be primitive, but it's magnificent—eastern Turkey has a romance found nowhere else. But you may have to suffer a bit—the summer sun is unrelenting and the winters harsh.

Discomforts here have to be borne stoically, with the thought that relatively few people travel this far east, so the experience is that much more of a privilege. Compensating factors include breathtaking scenery and extinct volcanoes that tower up to more than 5,000 metres (16,400 ft.).

And the region has its surprises: irregular rainfall gives occasional relief for the baked wasteland. In the south-eastern reaches is the strip of astonishing green that signifies the start of the Fertile Crescent—the sickle-shaped valley known as the cradle of civilization that leads all the way to the Persian Gulf.

The best way to see eastern Turkey is to base yourself at Erzurum and, depending on weather conditions, make arrangements from there—not forgetting that you need permission in writing from the government to visit certain areas near the border.

Erzurum

The mountains closing in on all sides hide the fact that the plain of Erzurum is almost 2,000 metres (6,562 ft.) above sea level, the highest in Anatolia. But there is no disguising it in winter.

The homes of the quarter of a million residents huddle together as if seeking protection. In the past, they needed it: Erzurum's position on the Silk Route may have brought riches, but it also led to battles for power. In its 6,000-year history, the city has fallen dozens of times to armies crossing Asia Minor. A turbulent enough record without the frequent earthquakes that have added to the damage over the years.

But even today, the Seljuk monuments still stand boldly, putting the awkward concrete apartment blocks to shame. One thing that takes the bite off winter is skiing—Erzurum boasts its own resort in the nearby hills.

The **Double Minaret Medrese** *(Çifte Minareli Medrese)*, in the centre of the old town, was built as a theological school in 1253. Blue ceramic squares decorate the brick minarets. On the right-hand one you'll see the double-

headed eagle, symbol of the Seljuk Turks. Cell-like study rooms line the courtyard on either side at ground- and first-floor level, where each group of students would be instructed in theology and positive sciences such as chemistry, medicine and mathematics by its religious teacher, a *müderris*.

At the far end, the **Tomb of Hatun** *(Hatuniye Türbesi)*, was constructed some 50 years earlier for the body of Hûdâvend Hatun, a daughter of the Seljuk sultan Alaettin Keykubat. The circular *türbe* was used for prayer and reading the Koran. Hatun's body was later removed, and that of a Turkish soldier was placed there in symbolic commemoration of the dead of World War I.

The *medrese* has been heavily restored, although outside only the ruins of the sleeping quarters remain. Crows wheeling above from the clump of poplar trees may distract your attention towards the outlying hills. The Ottoman fortifications are identified by the words "Mejidiye" and "Aziziye" on lime-painted stones below. The second one was the scene of bloody fighting in the War of Independence, marked by a ferocious-looking monument on the eastern edge of town.

Just beside the *medrese*, Erzurum's oldest mosque, the

Ulu Cami, dates from 1179. Coloured light bulbs strung across the top proclaim "There is no god but God; Muhammad is his Prophet". Parisian-style lamps at street level guide you to the entrance, helped by the twittering of nesting sparrows above the doorway.

Inside, you may be startled by the strip lighting that traces a fluorescent door to Mecca around the 800-year-old stone *mihrab.* Look up to see the crisscross beams of pine that replaced the dome after it collapsed in an earthquake.

Behind the mosque are the **Three Tombs** *(Üç Kümbetler),* thought to contain the bodies of a Seljuk emir and members of his family. The emir's is the one on an octagonal base.

Make your way past tumbledown homes of mud, stone and wood, which seem as old as the tombs, up to the **Fortress** *(Kale).* Two Russian cannon bear witness to the fortress's most recent military activity—its first was in Roman times during the 5th century. Muslim Arabs added to it, and Seljuk Turks also left their mark in the familiar pattern of occupation by constructing a *mesçit* (small tomb) with minaret —oddly, some 40 metres away. The conical roof of the tomb

bears a fuzzy covering of grass. The minaret was converted into a watch tower and the Ottomans added Gothic-style wooden columns at the top. A lightbulb profile of Atatürk keeps a watchful eye on the city from the ramparts, and you can look down, too, on grassed rooftops ideal for grazing sheep.

A second theological college, the **Yakutiye Medresesi,** is easily identified by its apparently missing minaret. The truncated left-hand column is capped by a conical roof. Note the two facing lions on the left of the porch and the double-headed eagle with its left head missing. On the other

side of the porch, more lions and again an eagle that has lost one of its heads, this time the right-hand one.

The **Lalapaşa Camii** was built in 1562 during the reign of Suleiman the Magnificent. Its distinctive styling—a central dome surrounded by four semi-domes and four smaller ones—leads some experts to believe it was the work of the Ottoman architect Sinan.

To round off a day's sightseeing, it's well worth browsing round the **Rüstempaşa Hanı,** a 16th-century inn that now has a bazaar built around it. Shop after shop offers necklaces, earrings and souvenir prayer beads made from *oltu taşı,* a black stone found in the Oltu district of Erzurum province. The original entrance to the inn is on a lower level.

The **Museum** *(Müze),* in Paşalar Caddesi, displays items ranging from Hittite to Ottoman. Among them are Ottoman cradles made from carpet wool and a *keçe,* the shepherd's cloak and thick woollen boots still worn in eastern Anatolia.

Pride of Erzurum's tourist sporting activities is the ski resort about 6 kilometres (4 mi.) south of town, **Palandöken Tesisleri.** Skiing is from just over 3,000

The further east you travel, the more austere the surroundings.

metres (9,842 ft.), and instruction, as well as equipment, is available from December to April—sometimes longer—in Turkey's "mini-Siberia" (Küçük Sibiriya).

Nemrut Daği

Of all the rulers who have aspired to immortality, King Antiochus I probably came closer than most to a place among the gods. Antiochus—born in the 1st century B.C.—ruled the tiny kingdom of Commagene, which bordered the west bank of the Euphrates river, east of present-day Malatya and Adıyaman. Since the kingdom was at peace with its neighbours, Antiochus had little else to occupy his mind with than preparations for his eventual ascent to a divine place. Choosing the highest mountain in northern Mesopotamia, Nemrut Daği, 2,150 metres (7,054 ft.), he replaced the top with a huge mound of earth and sandstone chips.

At the base of the mound, he placed 10-metre limestone statues of the gods seated on thrones consisting of 5-ton blocks of stone, facing due east and west to catch the first and last rays of the sun. Alongside the gods, of course, was Antiochus (he was already referring to himself as the God King). Sandstone reliefs were carved, portraying the king shaking hands with each god in turn—

these faced west to ensure his immediate transformation into a semi-divine being. The rest was just a matter of time. The north and south walls were taken up with other members of the royal family: facing north, father's side; facing south, mother's.

The most comfortable way of seeing sunset and sunrise from Nemrut Daği is to stay overnight at a hotel or *pansiyon* lower down the mountain, either on the Adıyaman side or at Büyüköz if you come from Malatya. That way, you can comfortably watch the sun go down and have a reasonable amount of sleep before getting up for the dawn ascent. Otherwise, it means setting out as early as 1.30 a.m. from Adıyaman for a bone-jarring 2½-hour mini-bus drive (be sure to check that you're paying the official price—you can easily find yourself overcharged). Having survived the ride, you may find that a biting pre-dawn easterly wind will penetrate all but the warmest of clothing. But in the eerie silence of dusk or dawn, the trip will be well worth it.

The final clamber to the summit isn't only for tourists. As the first hint of pink appears in the sky, you can see shapes huddling

Lonely heads, fissured and forlorn, prove that even the gods can tumble and fall.

140

in blankets in the darkness waiting, in accordance with Muslim law, before praying. Some are kneeling in readiness on flat slabs of rock.

Little that is identifiable remains of the gallery of gods. The heads have long since tumbled and are spread in random fashion on the ground, staring sightlessly towards the horizon as though blinded by centuries of exposure to the sun.

Even the tumulus has lost its stature: the use of dynamite to discover the whereabouts of Antiochus lowered the artificial mountaintop by a third. Antiochus has so far eluded everyone. Whether he made it to the skies is a matter of speculation. But in fairness to the Commagene king, even though his statue didn't withstand the rigours of time, his companions don't seem to have fared any better.

Van

A colourful carpet of flowers follows the banks of Turkey's biggest lake, Van Gölü, to the remains of the former capital of the Urartian kingdom, known in ancient times as Tuşpa.

Steps cut into the rock take you up to the **Citadel** *(Van Kalesi)*. As you ascend, note the cuneiform inscriptions dating from the early 9th century B.C., and some later ones dedicated to the

Persian ruler Xerxes. The burial chambers impart an air of sombreness matched by the view as you look out over the silent ruins of what was a prosperous lakeside city some 2,700 years ago.

Close to it, Van is a booming town of 100,000 people, renowned for its ornate rugs. Legacies of the Seljuk and Ottoman Turkish empires include the square-cut **Hüsrev Paşa Mosque** mirrored in the still waters, the minaret matching the sandwich slabs of the mosque walls. Van's **Museum** *(Müze)* has a fascinating selection of archaeological finds including utensils from as far back as the Early Bronze Age, and a collection of finely woven kilim rugs.

Van can be reached by road or rail, with a ferry connection from Tatvan, on the south-western edge of the lake. The 4-hour crossing, although longer than the drive, is a picturesque and relaxing way to approach Van. You can also better appreciate the size of the alkaline lake, which covers an area of 3,713 square kilometres (1,448 sq. mi.).

Beyond the formidable peak of Mt. Süphan, to the north-west, is **Malazgirt,** site of a

Such biblical scenes enhance the charm of modern Turkey.

historic battle that preceded Seljuk Turkish rule in Anatolia. The Seljuk and Byzantine armies clashed on a sweltering summer day in 1071. The Seljuk forces routed the Christians and took the whole of Anatolia into their empire.

A mirage in the middle of nowhere, Ishak Pasha Palace.

Mt. Ararat

A platform of cloud lifts the snowcapped peak 5,165 metres (16,946 ft.) into the sky—from any angle a stunning sight. If you drive past in a southerly direction from Iğdır, the peak splits into two at Doğubayazıt. The freezing summit of Büyük Ağrı (Great Ararat), where Noah's Ark is said to have come to rest, is more than 900 metres (3,000 ft.) higher

than its sister, Küçük Ağrı (Small Ararat).

Tackling the icy volcanic crater, which rises only a few miles from the Iranian border, is not for amateurs. Apart from anything else, you need an authorized guide, permission in writing and several days at your disposal to handle the grim ascent.

If you go simply to view the

majestic outline of Mt. Ararat, **Doğubayazıt** is worth visiting since it has another of eastern Anatolia's most arresting sights, the **Ishak Pasha Palace** *(Ishak Paşa Sarayı)*. On a clear or cloudy day, the view is unforgettable.

Perched on a hillside, southeast of Doğubayazıt, the palace and mosque overlook the sprawl of the town and the vast plain,

Elusive Ark

The prospect of finding the remains of Noah's Ark, whether fact or fantasy, has drawn dozens of adventurers to Mount Ararat.

The first man recorded as reaching the summit, the Estonian von Parrot, found no evidence of it in 1829. Eleven years later an earthquake and avalanche on the mountain wiped out a village built on the spot where Noah was said to have planted his first vineyard. The disaster also brought down an Armenian monastery and a chapel.

Other climbers have since tried with varying success to reach the top. Some brought back pieces of wood they claimed were from the Ark, but tests have indicated otherwise.

The search goes on, although local people don't think there is much chance: the popular belief is that the Ark is there, but God has ordained that no one shall see it.

145

Mount Ararat, said to be the cradle of the human race.

broken by craggy mountains. Ornate carvings in wood and stone show the mix of eastern styles prevalent in the 16th century, when work on the complex began. Of outstanding merit are the doors to the harem and the men's quarters. The main entrance door, made of gold, survived until World War I. Then, occupying Russian forces took it over the border and on from there to Moscow.

You can see the foundations of the original city, from the 1st millennium B.C. Across a pass is a ruined fortification thought to have been built around the same time. The mosque came more than 2,000 years later, when the Ottomans were expanding their empire.

WHAT TO DO

Sightseeing is just the beginning of a visit to Turkey. Eating out, shopping, entertainment—all spiced with a touch of the exotic—are authentic, even unexpected pleasures. And with such a lengthy coastline, offering every beach from the ultra-fashionable to the untouched, it's no surprise that water sports top the list of recreative pastimes.

Sports

Swimming. Istanbul's main hotels have swimming pools for guests. Non-guests can take out seasonal membership at the Etap Marmara and the Hilton.

The best beaches within reach of the city are the attractive Black Sea resorts of Şile and Kilyos. In summer a bus leaves Üsküdar for Şile every half hour from 7.30 a.m. to 6 p.m. For Kilyos, on the European side, catch the Bosphorus boat from Eminönü, disembark at Sarıyer, then hire a taxi or *dolmuş*.

There's swimming on the Princes Islands, too, but avoid the weekends and the crowds. The Bosphorus is not recommended for cleanliness; nor are the nearer beaches on the Sea of Marmara. Florya is a popular resort there, but slippery bright-green seaweed in the shallows may put you off. Further

along the northern Marmara, past Silivri, are far nicer white sand beaches, especially around Gümüşyaka and Sultanköy.

The Aegean and Mediterranean coasts offer innumerable opportunities for superb bathing. The choice is infinite, from popular holiday resorts to forgotten coves and thermal pools.

Boating. Whether you hire a craft or you're here under your own steam, the Aegean coast is the ideal place for boating enthusiasts. Hired vessels come with or without crew, but make your arrangements early—there aren't enough to go round. The celebrated Blue Voyage *(Mavi Yolculuk)* offers unrivalled opportunities for swimming, picnicking and sightseeing on shore. It's a yacht cruise organized by various agents, lasts a week and can be taken out of Kuşadası, Bodrum, Datça, Marmaris, or Fethiye and Kaş on the Mediterranean. Don't forget other cruise possibilities: maybe a full two weeks out of Istanbul along the Aegean and Mediterranean coasts.

The best boating season is May to October. In the summer the *meltem* or etesian wind blows from north-west to south-east on the Aegean, and can create choppy seas in the afternoon. It lasts about 40 days. Around Izmir and Kuşadası they call it the *imbat*.

Official sources advise that it's best to avoid zigzagging between Turkish and Greek waters. Archaeological finds should be left where they are: if discovered on board, the boat can be confiscated.

Fishing. Line and net fishing is permitted without a licence in any non-prohibited area (if in doubt, check with the local tourist office). Fishermen can always be found to take you out with them for a day's sport. Spear-fishing and scuba-diving are not allowed in Turkish waters.

Skiing. Uludağ near Bursa is the "in" place for winter sports, with chair-lifts, ski-tows, slalom and giant slalom courses, beginners' slopes, instruction and a fashionable après-ski scene. Equipment can be hired. The

season is January to April. You can also ski near Erzurum in eastern Turkey.

Larger Aegean resorts offer **wind-surfing** and **tennis.** In Istanbul, non-members are accepted at the Tacspor tennis club, Yenigelin Sokak. 2, Suadiye (coaching available).

Spectator Sports

The country's national speciality is **oil wrestling** *(yağlı güreş).* Edirne is the place to see it. Competitions are held in June, when muscular participants in leather pants, coated all over with oil, perform a ceremonial march before flinging each other around, to the cheers of thousands. Or, even more extraordinary, catch up with a bout of **camel wrestling** *(deve güreşi)* at Selçuk, near Kuşadası. Camels are far from sweet-tempered at the best of times. In this sport two moody males express mutual antagonism by sparring together until one is established as the victor, and the other is dragged off to get over the insult. It's exciting, and the animals are not exposed to serious injury.

After all that excitement, **horse-racing,** held at the Veliefendi Hippodrome near Bakırköy, some 15 kilometres (9 mi.) from Istanbul, might seem rather tame. Meetings take place from April to December, then horses and punters move to Izmir.

Shopping

Bazaars, markets and shops all over Turkey are full of exciting things to buy. Many of the goods make their way to Istanbul but some are better—and cheaper—in their own areas. Fixed prices are becoming more common but when you do bargain, bargain with firmness. You'll make friends, not lose them. And if you're offered tea or coffee during the process, accept it as a perfectly sincere gesture.

Carpets, of course, are at the top of the list. A quick distinction here: carpets are knotted, kilims are woven and have no pile. Both originated as floor and wall coverings for nomad dwellings; no two are alike. You can learn to "read" the symbols which convey such ideas as true love, protection against the Evil Eye or desire for a child. Age, rarity and (when applicable) the number of knots per square centimetre influence the price. Experts rely largely on touch to assess the quality of wool and silk and test whether dyes are chemical or natural.

Rarity apart, the most expensive are silk. A cheaper version exists, mixing silk and artificial fibres. These can make attractive wall hangings but won't stand up to use on the floor. You will see few really antique carpets and if you do come across one it will have to be cleared for export.

GÖREME VALLEY

The merchant should take care of the formalities. Many dealers are genuinely helpful, and should point out which are machine-made articles. The more you talk with them, the more likely you are to recognize real worth.

Turkish towels are renowned worldwide. They were invented in Bursa for a sybaritic sultan who wanted instant drying power when he left the bath. He organized a competition to find it. A Bursa man won, and Bursa still manufactures the best towels.

Handbeaten objects in **copper** and **brass** gleam from dozens of shops and workshops. Bakırcılar Caddesi in Istanbul's Beyazıt district is a good street to go looking. Turkish braziers are marvellously decorative and come in many shapes and sizes. Or what about launching out on a shoeshine box like the ones put to good use in the streets? Less weighty is the huge selection of lamps, candlesticks, coffeegrinders, long-handled pots for making Turkish coffee, and samovars. Turkish artisans will also take pride in crafting copper and brass objects to your own requirements.

Crystal is appealing and cheap,

If the pots are too heavy to carry, fly them home on a magic carpet.

ceramic plates make a pleasant souvenir and so do Turkish **tiles.** The best are old ones from Iznik, but in Bursa you'll be presented with a wide choice of new tiles in traditional blues and greens. **Onyx** turns up everywhere: the factory near Pergamum can create individual articles. **Meerschaum,** a white, claylike mineral, is carved into pipes and figurines. Or you could stun friends back home with a *nargile* (water pipe).

As for **jewellery,** the best finds are in the bazaars. Main fashion streets also have jewellery boutiques. Gold is normally sold by weight, with something added for workmanship. The current gold price is displayed by the shop; if in doubt you can check in the daily paper.

Some of the **textiles** are exquisite and so is the **embroidery.** Look for blouses in raw cotton *(şile bezi)* or headscarves *(yemeni)* edged with handmade lace *(oya).* Socks and stockings knitted in Central Anatolia carry bright designs. Small needlework purses represent hours of work.

Leather and **suede goods** offer bargains for men and women, and the quality of the skins is superb. You can have shoes custom-made by small craftsmen; more typical is the bejewelled Turkish slipper.

All sorts of **spices,** including henna and snuff, are for sale in Istanbul's Spice Market, where you can also unearth herbal pick-me-ups.

You will run across a fair number of **antiques** including coins, glassware, samovars and Ottoman pieces. A small flea market springs up near the Istanbul Book Market every Sunday. Some shops specialize in taking elements of antique Turkish jewellery and working them into attractive necklaces, bracelets and earrings. Usually silver, they're often enhanced with niello. Of course, you have to keep an eye out for reproductions, and if you're offered a "Byzantine icon", take it with a pinch of salt.

And, to appeal to a variety of tastes and budgets, there are imitation swords and daggers, *karagöz* marionettes traditionally cut from camel parchment, blue beads to protect you against the Evil Eye or Muslim prayer-beads *(tespih)* in every imaginable material, including plastic, olivewood and agate. Or maybe you could learn to play the *saz,* the musical instrument resembling a mandolin. Pamukkale produces an intriguing souvenir: statuettes are soaked in mineral water until they become coated with lime. At Kuşadası, Bodrum and Marmaris you'll see sponges in all shapes and sizes, while Bodrum's hand-crafted leather sandals are chic, cool and practical.

Entertainment

Belly-dancing is typically oriental, and every Turkish girl can do it. As performed by the best dancers, scantily clad in shimmering gauze, it's subtle, graceful and erotic. There are certain basic figures, but generally the girls invent as they go along, pivoting the lower part of the body, scooping up their long hair, using a horizontal head movement and accompanying it all with constant arm and hand gestures to the sound of small cymbals. The top performers are at the top night-spots, hence the most expensive.

Floorshows with a tourist slant will also include folk dances which vary according to their regions of origin. You may see the *Horon*, a Black Sea dance where men clad in black and silver quiver like fishes caught in a net to the music of a primitive violin, or maybe the Sword and Shield Dance of Bursa, depicting the Ottoman conquest of the city, enacted to the clash of weapons. Clacking wooden spoons provide the rhythm for the lively Spoon Dance *(Kaşik Oyunu)*.

Turkish-style supper clubs *(gazino)* provide Turkish dancing, music and a programme of assorted performers; a *taverna* is similar, usually with a more exuberant atmosphere. Discos and nightclubs are much like their Western counterparts. Turks

seize any occasion for dancing, usually to a cocktail of Western and Turkish music, although they're at their most uninhibited with the latter. Trying is the best way to learn the national style of dance, but it helps to have a Turkish partner to imitate.

Turkish music falls into several categories: folk songs, classical compositions, largely from the 18th century, and the popular westernized type you hear on the radio. The annual Istanbul Festival (mid-June to mid-July) gives summer visitors the occasion to enjoy a variety of artistic offerings. Tickets are sold at the Atatürk Cultural Centre, Taksim Square. Don't miss rousing displays by the Military Band, presented most days at the Military Museum. The brilliantly garbed performers play kettledrums, clarinets, cymbals and bells with a gusto that sets your ears ringing. The Istanbul State Opera reaches a high standard in a repertoire of Western and Turkish works, performed from October to May at the Atatürk Centre. There, too, during the same period, are regular concerts by the Istanbul State Symphony Orchestra, recitals by Turkish and foreign artists and performances by the State Ballet.

Turks excel at backgammon *(tavla)*, and almost any coffeehouse produces a formidable crop of players. However, coffee-

houses are considered a "men only" preserve. That effectively precludes women from having a go at water pipe smoking. Lots of coffee-houses have pipes for hire and will prepare one.

All through the summer, musical festivals bring gaiety to the streets.

There are seven casinos in the country, where you'll find most of the usual games.

Don't leave without trying a Turkish bath, preferably in one of the famous baths like Cağaloğlu Hamamı in Yerebatan Cad-desi, an 18th-century beauty well used to foreigners, or the even older (16th-century) Galatasaray Hamamı, in Istanbul. The experience is sensuous, cleansing and relaxing, but the architecture alone makes a visit worthwhile.

Note there are usually separate entrances for men *(erkekler)* and women *(kadınler),* but sometimes special hours or days are designated. You undress in a cubicle, then, enveloped in a towel, proceed via a steamy side-room to the centre slab in the hot room, where you are rubbed down by the attendant with a special bath mitt to remove impurities from the skin. If the treatment is too enthusiastic you have only to indicate, and, should the heat become oppressive, you can escape into a cooler room. Thus steamed, honed, massaged and probably a few pounds lighter, you emerge feeling on top of the world.

Festivities

Except in February and March, when the weather is often wet and miserable, there is something going on somewhere all the time. As dates vary, check with the tourist office if you don't want to miss something special.

January *Selçuk* (Ephesus) and *Aydin,* south of Izmir: Camel wrestling.

April *Manisa* Powergum Festival, when a traditional local remedy, *mesir macunu,* is brewed. *Istanbul* Tulip Festival.

May *Konya* javelin-throwing from horseback (every weekend until October). *Selçuk* (Ephesus) Festival of Culture and Art, some concerts taking place in the ancient theatre at Ephesus. *Bergama* Festival of Pergamum: drama, folk dancing, crafts.

June *Izmir* International Mediterranean Festival. *Konya* Rose-growing Competiton. *Marmaris* Music and Art Festival. *Edirne* Oil Wrestling Tournament. *Istanbul* International Festival of art and culture, lasting until mid-July.

July *Bursa* Folklore and Music Festival, Trade and Tourism Fair. *Foça* Music, Folklore and Water Sports Festival.

August *Çanakkale* Troy Festival, folk dancing and music. *Izmir* International Fair.

September *Bodrum* Culture and Art, with classical music concerts in Bodrum Castle, art and water sports. *Kirşehir* Ahi Evran Crafts and Folklore Festival. *Çorum* (near Ankara) Hittite Festival. *Cappadocia* Tourism Festival. *Mersin* Textile and Fashion Fair. *Diyarbakır* Water melon Festival. *Konya* Cooking Competition.

October *Antalya* Film and Art Festival. *Konya* Turkish Troubador's Week.

December *Aydin* province, Camel wrestling. *Demre* St. Nicholas Festival. *Konya* Mevlana Festival, with Whirling Dervish dancers.

EATING OUT

Gastronomes rank Turkish cuisine as one of the best in the world. It's inexpensive by most standards, and customers are invariably treated with courtesy in even the smallest restaurant. In many places, it is customary to enter the kitchen and point out what you want to eat.

The setting is often as memorable as the meal, especially if you dine outdoors along the sea shore. A starry sky, a whisper of oriental music, vines shadowing old stone walls, the lapping of water nearby and, if you're lucky, a moon big enough to look as though it's hired for the occasion.

Starters

Meze is the name given to an enormous selection of appetizers, both hot and cold. They can represent a meal in themselves, so until you feel in the swing of things, avoid ordering a main dish until you've sampled them.

Cold *meze* are usually presented on a tray at your table for selection. Try stuffed mussels, Turkish pastrami cured with red pepper, chopped cucumber and yoghurt pepped up with garlic, smoked oxtongue, mashed fava beans.

Dolma means stuffed vegetables—usually peppers, aubergines, tomatoes or vine leaves.

Good Turkish bread or *pide* (unleavened bread) adds to your enjoyment of a variety of dips: maybe fish roe mixed with lemon juice and oil *(tarama)*, grilled aubergine whipped with lemon or yoghurt *(patlıcan salatası)* or thyme-flavoured yoghurt *(haydariye)*. Traditionally, *rakı* is drunk with them all.

Perhaps you'd prefer hot entrées like spiced mutton liver *(arnavut ciğeri)*, wafer-thin pastries stuffed with cheese or minced meat *(muska böreği)* or fried mussels *(midye tava)*.

Soups

What about soup: "wedding soup" *(düğün çorbası)*, lamb broth flavoured with lemon, thickened with beaten egg; red lentil soup *(kırmızı mercimek çorbası)*; or mutton tripe soup *(işkembe çorbası)*? Turks swear by this one as a remedy for a hangover.

Fish

When they tell you the fish is fresh, they mean it. You can run the gamut from swordfish *(kılıç)*, bluefish *(lüfer)*, tunny *(palamut)*, mackerel *(uskumru)* and red mullet *(barbunya)* to sardines and anchovies. In Istanbul the smart fish restaurants are at Tarabya on the Bosphorus, but they're good anywhere in the city and along the coasts. Seafood, also delicious, is expensive.

Main Courses

Kebabs are a speciality: *şiş kebap* is lamb and tomatoes served with rice. Lamb and beef roasted on a vertical skewer, then thinly sliced, is called *döner kebap*. There are various meat and vegetable stews, easier to identify on the spot in the kitchen than by their names on the menu.

Vegetarians will be in their element—there are so many meatless dishes that you don't need to look for a special restaurant. Rice pilaf *(pilav)* is satisfying, cracked wheat pilaf *(bulgur pilavı)* even more so.

Desserts

You'll think you're back in the harem when you come to the desserts. "Lips of the beloved" *(dilber dudağı)* and "lady's navel" *(hanım göbeği)* are both fried delicacies. Nightingale's Nest *(bülbül yuvası)*, walnut-stuffed pastry, is shaped like its namesake; familiar *baklava* is a pastry with walnuts or pistachio nuts. All are served with syrup.

Highly recommended are the milk puddings and various sweetmeats. Turkish Delight *(lokum)* is the best-known, but there's also *helva* which represents a whole category of sweets in Turkey. And, of course, delicious fruit: ripe peaches, plump nectarines, yellow melons from Çeşme, strawberries, pears, cherries and grapes.

The hazelnuts and almonds are excellent. Turks like their almonds served unroasted and chilled. You'll see pedlars wheeling their wares past restaurants at night, with the almonds laid out on a block of ice and a flaming gas lamp to light the way.

Beverages

Rakı, an aniseed liqueur, can be drunk throughout the meal either neat or with water, whereupon it assumes a pearly colour. Half-and-half is a reasonable mixture for beginners; advanced students could test themselves on beer and *rakı,* popular with Turkish soldiers. Beer consumption is high, the quality good. Locally produced vodka, cognac, whisky and gin are an honourable and less expensive substitute for imported brands.

Turkish wines *(şarap)* have a tradition going back to 7000 B.C.; European vine-stocks may well originally have come from here. Nevertheless, despite the quality products available, Turks are not great wine drinkers, and only a small proportion of the harvest goes into wine-making and from there onto the home market. Still, there's a full range of reds, rosés, whites and sparkling wines; the standard is high, sometimes exceptional. The same is true of liqueurs with a fruit, coffee or cocoa base. Sour cherry *(vişne)* is especially delectable.

Of course, you may well settle for bottled water, in which case remember that here "mineral" water *(maden suyu)* means the fizzy variety. Beverage specialities are refreshing *ayran*, yoghurt whipped with water, and *boza*, a calorie-packed sourish drink made from fermented millet, at its best in pudding shops where it's served sprinkled with cinnamon.

Coffee *(kahve)* means Turkish coffee, strong and well-brewed, poured grounds and all into tiny cups without milk or cream. Specify the degree of sweetness you want when you order: *sade* (without sugar), *az şekerli* (slightly sweetened), *orta şekerli* (sweet), or *çok şekerli* (very sweet). Leave it a minute to let the grounds settle.

Tea *(çay)* is grown near the Black Sea and, served throughout the day in waisted glasses, it's the cup of friendship, drunk hot and strong without milk.

Snacks

Sample a round sesame-seed roll *(simit)*, sold from little stalls and trays wherever you go. Corn on the cob is another kerbside treat. Pizza bars are springing up everywhere; the real Turkish-style pizza is the *Karadeniz pidesi* originating in the Black Sea area. On the Aegean Coast you'll find that cucumbers *(salatalık)* are a great thirst-quencher. Barrow salesmen peel them, you salt and pepper to taste. Or bite into a slice of watermelon *(karpuz)*. Ice creams, sherbets and cakes are all highly recommended. Naturally, buy only from stalls where the hygiene seems up to standard.

Döner kebap, the Turkish takeaway... and dainties fit for a pasha.

BERLITZ-INFO

CONTENTS

A Accommodation   162
(hotels, flats, motels, holiday villages, boarding houses,
youth hostels)

Airports   163

Antiquities   163

C Camping   163

Car Hire   164

Climate   164

Clothing   165

Communications (post offices, telegrams, telephone)   165

Consulates and Embassies   166

Conversion Charts   167

Courtesies   168

Crime and Theft   168

Customs and Entry Formalities   168

D Driving (entering Turkey, speed limits,   169
driving conditions, traffic police, accidents, breakdowns,
distance measurements, road signs)

E Emergencies   172

G Getting to Turkey (by air, sea, rail, bus, car)   172

Guides   173

H	Health and Medical Care	173
	Hitch-hiking	174
L	Language	174
M	Maps	175
	Money Matters	175
	(currency, banks, eurocheques, traveller's cheques, credit cards)	
N	Newspapers and Magazines	176
P	Police	176
	Prices	176
	Public Holidays	177
R	Restaurants	178
S	Shopping	178
T	Time Differences	178
	Tipping	179
	Toilets	179
	Tourist Information Offices	179
	Transport	180
	(buses, taxis, dolmuş, ferries, long-distance buses, trains, planes)	
W	Water	181

A ACCOMMODATION

See also CAMPING. The Turkish Ministry of Culture and Tourism has rated some of the hotels, motels and boarding houses from luxury to fourth class. Those with top rating offer the maximum comfort on a par with international standards. Many other establishments, especially on the Aegean Coast, are checked by municipal authorities. However, if you are planning to travel way off the tourist beat, you'll probably have to content yourself with unclassified and simple—if not primitive—lodging, so bring your own linen or sleeping bag.

Many hotels make only an extra-bed charge for children sharing a room with their parents. Check whether breakfast, VAT (12 %) and service charge (15 %) are included in the room rate.

Hotels *(otel).* Most big towns have either first- or second-class hotels. Luxury establishments are virtually confined to Ankara, Istanbul, Bursa, Izmir, Antalya and Adana. In every case, refer to the hotel guide published by the Ministry of Culture and Tourism, available at tourist information offices.

Flats/Apartments *(apartman dairesi)* and **villas** *(villa),* furnished and unfurnished, are cheaper than a hotel room for long stays. Watch for the sign "Kiralık" ("For Hire") or contact an estate agent (broker).

Motels *(motel)* fall into three categories. They are nearly always equipped with shower, toilet and a radio; some include air-conditioning and a fridge. Normally they sleep two people, but managements are generally cooperative about putting in extra beds for children, or you can hire two units side by side and open them into a suite for families.

Holiday villages *(tatil köyleri)* in seaside areas, classed A and B, provide furnished flats—sometimes, but not always, with cooking facilities. They all have a shop and restaurant close at hand, and most have a swimming pool.

Boarding houses *(pansiyon)* offer a more intimate glimpse of Turkish life. Breakfast is included in the price, and there may be a kitchen where you can cook and share a fridge. Toilets and bathroom are usually communal. Cheapest of all is a dormitory where you share the room with up to five others.

Youth hostels *(talebe yurdu)* offer benefits to holders of International Student Travel Conference (ISTC) or International Youth Hostel Federation (IYHF) cards and visitors with "student" or "teacher" on their passport. (Note that ISTC cards also allow reductions on Turkish domestic and international flights, domestic and international maritime lines, trains, and on entrance to museums, cinemas and concerts.) Youth hostels are generally open between July and September.

I'd like a single/double room.	Tek/Çift yataklı bir oda istiyorum.
with bath/shower	banyolu/duşlu
What's the rate per night?	Bir gecelik oda ücreti ne kadar?

AIRPORTS (havaalanı)

Ankara. Esenboğa, 35 km. (22 mi.) outside the city, is reached by taxi in only 20 minutes, by bus slightly more. It has all the usual airport facilities.

Istanbul. All international and domestic flights land at Atatürk Hava Limanı, 23 km. (15 mi.) out of town. Turkish Airlines (THY, *Türk Hava Yolları*) run a regular bus service from the airport to Bakırköy, Aksaray and Şişhane Air Terminal in central Istanbul.

Izmir. Çiğli Airport is 25 km. (16 mi.) from the city. Buses run to the THY Terminal, and minibuses take you from the centre of town to the waterfront depot right by the Tourist Information Office and city bus terminal. Taxis and *dolmuş* are also available.

Porter, please!	Hamal, lütfen!
Take these bags to the bus/ taxi, please.	Lütfen bu çantaları otobüse/ taksiye götürün.

ANTIQUITIES (antika eşya)

The purchase of antiquities is strictly prohibited, so make sure that the treasure you have acquired is not classified as an object of historical value, liable to be confiscated at customs and a potential source of trouble. Be prepared to show a bill on departure. Old coins are particularly protected. The merchant from whom you buy should be able to advise on all the formalities.

CAMPING (kamping) C

Campsites registered with the Ministry of Culture and Tourism are limited in number but generally offer showers and toilets, kitchen and laundry facilities, a shop and electricity. They are open April/May to October. Especially recommended are the sites operated by the Mocamp-Kervansaray, which are also licensed by the Ministry. You may camp outside organized sites provided you make yourself known to village authorities and, of course, request permission from the owner to set up on private land. But it is wiser to choose a place where there are other campers. Tourist information offices will help.

Can we camp here?	**Burada kamp yapabilir miyiz?**

CAR HIRE *(araba kiralama)*

See also DRIVING. International and local car-hire firms have offices in the major cities, as well as representatives at the international airports. Ask in advance about reduced rates for three- or four-week rentals, or any special seasonal deals. The main cars for hire are the *Fiat/Murat 124* and *131*, and *Renault 12,* which are all assembled in Turkey.

To hire a car, the driver must have a valid driving licence, and an International Driving Permit is recommended. Depending on the company and the car, the minimum age is 19, 21, 25 or 28. A deposit is usually required unless you pay by credit card. If a second person is to drive the car, permission should be requested from the rental agency when the car is taken out, otherwise the insurance is void.

In view of the state of some roads in Turkey, it doesn't do any harm to ask the agency to check that the car is in sound condition.

Independent travellers should look into the "Fly-and-Drive" programmes offered by various travel agencies.

CLIMATE

The best periods to visit Turkey are spring and autumn. The Marmara, Aegean and Mediterranean regions have hot summers; winters are mild on the Mediterranean coast. Seasonal showers are encountered near the Black Sea, and in some parts of Anatolia thunderstorms can break out suddenly—the open-umbrella road signs mean just that. Istanbul's rainy season is normally confined to January/February. In eastern Turkey, summers can be scorching, winters bitterly cold. Some average temperatures in degrees Fahrenheit:

		J	F	M	A	M	J	J	A	S	O	N	D
Ankara	max.	39	42	51	63	73	78	86	87	78	69	57	43
	min.	24	26	31	40	49	53	59	59	52	44	37	29

		J	F	M	A	M	J	J	A	S	O	N	D
Istanbul	max.	46	47	51	60	69	77	82	82	76	68	59	51
	min.	37	36	38	45	53	60	65	66	61	55	48	41
Izmir	max.	55	57	63	70	79	87	92	92	85	76	67	58
	min.	39	40	43	49	56	63	69	69	62	55	49	42
Samsun	max.	50	51	54	59	67	74	79	80	75	69	62	55
	min.	38	38	40	45	53	60	65	65	61	56	49	43

And in degrees Celsius:

		J	F	M	A	M	J	J	A	S	O	N	D
Ankara	max.	4	6	11	17	23	26	30	31	26	21	14	6
	min.	-4	-3	-1	4	9	12	15	15	11	7	3	-2
Istanbul	max.	8	9	11	16	21	25	28	28	24	20	15	11
	min.	3	2	3	7	12	16	18	19	16	13	9	5
Izmir	max.	13	14	17	21	26	31	33	33	29	24	19	14
	min.	4	4	6	9	13	17	21	21	17	13	9	6
Samsun	max.	10	11	12	15	19	23	26	27	24	21	17	13
	min.	3	3	4	7	12	16	18	18	16	13	9	6

Minimum temperatures are measured just before sunrise, maximum temperatures in the afternoon.

CLOTHING

Casual, light clothes are the answer for the coast, with something stylish for dining and dancing. Hats, sunglasses and tough shoes are a must for archaeological sites. A certain formality is expected in cities, where Turks dress up more in the evenings. The nights can turn chilly, so a sweater or jacket is advisable. Further east, you'll need at least an anorak, particularly if undertaking the dawn trip to Nemrut Dağı, where the mountain peak can be bitterly cold. Slip in an umbrella, and also some cream for the occasional mosquito around Silifke and some parts of the south coast.

When visiting mosques, you should always remove your shoes. Revealing tops, mini-skirts and shorts are unsuitable; women should cover their heads and arms. Sometimes scarves are provided, but it's a good idea to carry one on you.

COMMUNICATIONS

Post offices *(postane)* are identified by the letters PTT *(Posta, Telefon, Telgraf)* in black on a yellow background. City post offices and those of many towns are open 24 hours a day—weekends included—for telephoning and sometimes also sending telegrams and changing money. For other services, they may be open till 8 p.m. Smaller offices are open Monday to Saturday only until 5 or 6 p.m. and may close for lunch. Poste restante (general delivery) letters should be sent addressed care of the central post office *(Merkez Postanesi)* of the town you are travelling to. Large hotels have post offices or will handle your mail at the reception desk. *Pul* means stamps.

Street post boxes *(posta kutusu)* are yellow. The words *yurt dişi* mean "abroad", *yurt içi* "inland" and *şehir içi* "local".

Telegrams for foreign countries can be sent normal or urgent *(acele)*; there is also a lightning service *(yıldırım)* for destinations within Turkey. However, it can be cheaper, and just as fast, to use the Telefax service *(faksimil mektup)* available at city post offices.

Telephone. Tokens *(jeton)* for public telephones are sold at post offices and sometimes by dealers outside. There are three sizes: *büyük, normal* and *küçük* (large, medium and small). The first two are suitable for long-distance and international calls, the third for phoning locally. Where you see only *büyük* and *küçük*, middle-sized tokens count as large.

For international calls, lift the receiver, insert a token and dial 9. When you hear the buzzing tone, dial another 9 followed by the country code. When you hear rapid pips on the line, it's time to insert another token.

Avoid making calls from Turkish hotels, for you may be charged 50% or more commission. It's generally much cheaper to ring from a call box, and quicker, too, as operator-connected calls abroad can take an hour or so to come through.

Have you received any mail for me?	**Bana posta var mı acaba?**
A stamp for this letter/ postcard, please.	**Bu mektup/kart için bir pul, lütfen.**
airmail/registered	**uçak ile/taahütlü**
I want to send a telegram to ...	**... (ya) bir telgraf yollamak istiyorum.**

CONSULATES and EMBASSIES *(konsolosluk, elçilik)*
If problems should develop, get in touch with your consulate or embassy:

Australia	Embassy: Nene Hatun Caddesi 83, Gaziosman-paşa, Ankara; tel. (4) 1361240
Canada	Honorary consul general: Mr Yavuz Kireç, Büyükdere Caddesi, Bengün Han 107, Kat 3 Kayrettepe, Istanbul; tel. (1) 1725174
	Embassy: Nene Hatun Caddesi 75, Gaziosman-paşa, Ankara; tel. (4) 1361275
Eire	Honorary consul general: Mr Ferruh Verdi, Cumhuriyet Caddesi, Pegasus Evi 26a, Harbiye; tel. (1) 1466025.
	The nearest embassy is in Rome.
New Zealand	The nearest embassy/consulate is in Athens; U.K. consulate in Istanbul will advise if necessary.
South Africa	The nearest embassy/consulate is in Athens.
U.K.	Consulate: Meşrutiyet Caddesi 34, Tepebaşı, Beyoğlu, Istanbul; tel. (1) 1447540
	Embassy: Şehit Ersan Caddesi 46a, Çankaya, Ankara; tel. (4) 1274310
U.S.A.	Consulate: Meşrutiyet Caddesi 104–108, Tepe-başı, Beyoğlu, Istanbul; tel. (1) 1513602
	Atatürk Bulvarı 110, Kavaklıdere, Ankara; tel. (4) 1265470

CONVERSION CHARTS

For distance measures, see DRIVING. Turkey uses the metric system.

Temperature

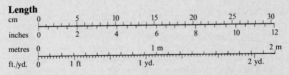

Length

Weight

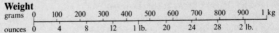

COURTESIES

You don't need to be stiffly polite, but old-world courtesy still prevails in this rather formal society, and circumspect behaviour wins friends. City dwellers are more relaxed than people in smaller places; try to understand and accept patterns of behaviour. For instance, women are not really welcome in coffee houses. Family values are upheld. Revealing clothing creates an unfortunate impression and can provoke antagonism. If something doesn't go your way, irritation and raised voices are less effective than quiet insistence.

From the poorest to the richest, Turks traditionally treat visitors as honoured guests. Hospitality is generous, spontaneous and sincere. Offers of cigarettes, tea and coffee will probably occur several times a day; feel free to accept and respond in kind. When visiting a private house, you may be invited to remove your shoes. Flowers or perfume are appropriate gifts for the hostess. Letters of thanks, a postcard or photographs are naturally appreciated.

In mosques, keep a respectful distance from people at prayer.

CRIME and THEFT

Aggression towards visitors is rare. However, pickpockets (men and women) of considerable talent and originality sometimes work in crowded places. One of their favourite ruses is starting a minor scuffle to attract your attention. Moral: deposit valuables in the hotel safe.

Keep a photocopy of your plane tickets and other personal documents, with a note of the phone and telex numbers of your travel agent: they could come in useful in case of loss or theft.

Drug offences, even minor involvement, are punishable by extremely severe prison sentences. Black-market moneychangers should be avoided.

CUSTOMS and ENTRY FORMALITIES

See also DRIVING. Most visitors, including British and American, need only a valid passport to enter Turkey; British subjects can even travel on the simplified Visitor's Passport. South African nationals require a visa. No vaccination certificates are needed.

Valuable items including jewellery, tape recorders, transistor radios and similar objects should be registered in your passport on entry, to ensure they can be taken out again when you leave. The purchase and export of antiquities is prohibited.

The following chart shows what main duty-free items you may take into Turkey and, upon your return home, into your own country:

Into:	Cigarettes		Cigars		Tobacco	Spirits	Wine
Turkey	400	or	50	or	200 g.	5 l.*	
Australia	200	or	250 g.	or	250 g.	1 l.	or 1 l.
Canada	200	and	50	and	900 g.	1.1 l.	or 1.1 l.
Eire	200	or	50	or	250 g.	1 l.	and 2 l.
N. Zealand	200	or	50	or	250 g.	1.1 l.	and 4.5 l.
S. Africa	400	and	50	and	2350 g.	1 l.	and 2 l.
U.K.	200	or	50	or	250 g.	1 l.	and 2 l.
U.S.A.	200	and	100	and	**	1 l.	or 1 l.

*in opened bottles, 3 l. of which may be whisky
**A reasonable quantity

Currency restrictions. Any amount of local or foreign currency may be imported. However, foreign currencies should be specified in the passport upon arrival in order to avoid difficulties on departure. Local currency up to the equivalent of U.S.$1,000, and foreign currencies up to the amount imported, may be taken out of the country.

Keep exchange slips since you may need to present them when reconverting Turkish money into foreign currency and when taking souvenirs out, as proof that the goods were purchased with legally converted currency.

I've nothing to declare. **Deklare edecek birşeyim yok.**

DRIVING   D

Entering Turkey. To bring your car into Turkey you will need:
- a valid driving licence or an International Driving Permit
- car registration papers
- a nationality plate or sticker
- international insurance certificate (Green Card) or alternatively third-party insurance. *Note:* make sure it covers both the European and Asian parts of Turkey.

Since you'll probably be travelling through other countries on your way to Turkey, find out about their national regulations, too, at your local automobile association and insurance company. For stays exceeding three months, you will need to apply to the Turkish Touring and Automobile Club (*Türkiye Turing ve Otomobil Kurumu,* TTOK) for a triptyque or *carnet de passage.*

When you cross the Turkish border, your passport must be stamped and the car registered in the passport.

In Turkey, the use of seat belts is compulsory. You must carry *two* red-reflector warning triangles and a first-aid kit. The blood alcohol limit is a strictly enforced zero; police controls are frequent throughout the country. Motorcycle riders and passengers must wear crash helmets.

Speed limits are 50 k.p.h. (31 m.p.h.) in urban areas, 90 k.p.h. (56 m.p.h.) on the open road. Cars towing caravans (trailers) are restricted to 40 k.p.h. (25 m.p.h.) and 80 k.p.h. (50 m.p.h.) respectively. Drive carefully, as Turks tend to disregard the limits.

Driving conditions. Roads around Istanbul and other main tourist areas are asphalted and well maintained. Elsewhere, it is a different story. Miles of secondary roads, and many stretches of main road, are unsuitable for any but the hardiest of cars and drivers. The official tourist map—one of the handiest, and free—shows most stretches under repair, describing them euphemistically as "stabilized".

It is strongly advisable to wear a seat belt (in any case, it is compulsory). After dark, the dangers multiply. Donkey carts will loom unlit from the shadows, and cyclists can easily approach on the wrong side without lights—on dual carriageways, too.

Traffic police, accidents. In the event of an accident, the police must be informed immediately *whether anyone has been injured or not;* the law requires that a police report be filed. Traffic police are understanding with foreigners but strict about speeding and drunken driving. You can be fined on the spot. Radar control is used on highways.

Breakdowns. Mechanics in Turkey are highly skilled and carry an unbelievable choice of spare parts, due to the fact that they spend a lot of time patching up the older cars you still see on the roads. However, since some foreign models may stump them, carry any parts you feel you may need. If you have the misfortune to break down, someone will almost certainly pull up to lend a hand or at least give you a lift to the nearest garage. Of the many vehicle repair workshops you'll see, *Oto Lastik* is for tyres, *Oto Elektrik* for wiring and *Oto Eksoz* exhaust systems. The Turkish Touring and Automobile Club will help you get repairmen.

For the **Istanbul** area they are at Halaskargazi Caddesi 364, Şişli; tel. (1) 131 46 31

For **Ankara**: Yenişehir, Adakale Sok. 4/11; tel. (4) 131 76 48

For **Izmir**: Atatürk Bulvarı 370; tel. (51) 21 71 49

If you are a holder of a letter of credit or traveller's protection cover from your home automobile association, the TTOK will make the necessary repairs and send the bill to your home country. The TTOK gives road assistance to members of FIA or AIT motoring organizations and pays the cost of transporting a damaged vehicle to the motorist's home country.

Note: If it is necessary to leave a vehicle behind in Turkey, it must be brought to the nearest customs office or local administrative authority to have the registration of the vehicle cancelled in your passport; only then will you be free to leave the country.

Fluid measures

imp.gals. 0 ——————————— 5 ——————————— 10

litres 0 — 5 — 10 ——— 20 ——— 30 ——— 40 ——— 50

U.S.gals. 0 ——————————— 5 ——————————— 10

Kilometres to miles

km 0 1 2 3 4 5 6 8 10 12 14 16

miles 0 ½ 1 1½ 2 3 4 5 6 7 8 9 10

Road signs. Most road signs are the standard pictographs used throughout Europe. However, you will encounter many written signs:

Azami park 1 saat	*Parking allowed for 1 hour*
Bozuk yol/satıh	*Poor surface*
Dikkat	*Caution*
Dur	*Stop*
Durmak yasaktır	*No stopping*
Düsük banket	*Low verge*
Gümrük	*Customs*
Kaygan yol	*Slippery road*
Park yapılmaz	*No parking*
Tamirat	*Roadworks*
Yavaş	*Slow down*

Are we on the right road for...?	... için doğru yolda mıyız?
Full tank, please.	Doldurun, lütfen.
normal/super/diesel	normal/süper/motorin
Check the oil/tyres/battery, please.	Yağı/Havayı/Aküyü kontrol edebilir misiniz, lütfen.
I've had a breakdown.	Arabam arzalandı.
There's been an accident.	Bir kaza oldu.

E EMERGENCIES

Your first requirement will be somebody who speaks English. Emergency telephone numbers are listed on the first page of directories. Depending on the type of emergency, refer to other entries in this section such as CONSULATES, HEALTH AND MEDICAL CARE, etc.

G GETTING TO TURKEY

By air. Istanbul has the major international airport in Turkey (see also p. 163), with services from Europe, the Middle East and the U.S.A. There are, however, also direct international flights into Izmir and Ankara. Flights from South Africa, Australia and New Zealand connect via various European cities. Many tour operators offer traditional air-and-hotel packages to Turkey, mainly to Istanbul and the Aegean and Mediterranean coastal resorts, sometimes including cruises and "adventure" trips through regions of historical interest.

By sea. There are regular car-ferry services to Istanbul and Izmir from Venice, Ancona, Famagusta (Cyprus) and many of the Greek Islands, as well as between Brindisi and Izmir or Ancona and Bodrum. In summer, there is also a 7-day Venice–Istanbul–Venice car/cruise service.

By rail. Direct daily trains run from Munich to Istanbul, with sleeping cars as far as Belgrade. The journey is long (1½ days), uncomfortable, smoky, crowded, but cheap. Another train leaves Venice in the late afternoon and arrives in Belgrade the next morning. You then have a long wait for the afternoon train to Istanbul, 26 hours away.

By bus. Several companies operate regular bus servics from cities in Europe (Athens, Hamburg, Munich, Paris, Vienna, etc.) to Istanbul. From Munich, an express bus makes the journey in about 40 hours.

By car. A new (incomplete) motorway whisks you across Yugoslavia as far as Niš, but you have to pay a toll on it. From there you can choose to cross Bulgaria (Sofia, Plovdiv, Edirne), which requires a transit visa, or take the longer route through Greece (Skopje, Salonica, Kavala, Ipsala). Your automobile association is the best source of advice. For driving regulations in Turkey, see pp. 169–171.

GUIDES
Travel agents are obliged to employ guides on all tours. Official guides wearing a black and white badge can be found at the entrance to some major sites; they work for a set fee. You can also arrange to hire a guide from the local tourist office. Sometimes, archaeologists and academics agree to act as guides. The local museum will know. For direction-finding, children will often apear and offer to take you to places of interest. A tip is in order.

HEALTH and MEDICAL CARE   H
There are no vaccination requirements. Take out adequate travel insurance to cover any risk of illness and accident while on holiday. Your travel agent or insurance company at home will be able to advise you.

Large hotels have doctors on call. Medical standards are high, but since there are long queues at public hospitals, it would be best to contact a private hospital in case of need. There is an American hospital in several cities:

Ankara: Balgat Amerikan Tesisleri; tel. (4) 133 70 80

Istanbul: Güzelbahçe Sok. 20, Nişantaşı; tel. (1) 131 40 50

Izmir: Eylül Üniversitesi Yanı 9; tel. (51) 22 45 00

Many doctors (as well as dentists and chemists) speak a language other than Turkish.

Stomach upsets are the most common problem for tourists. It's best to wash and peel all fruit and vegetables. Don't be too ready to sample cooked food (except *simit*) from street vendors.

Take the sun in easy doses at first (only 15 minutes direct exposure for the first day or two) and avoid heat exhaustion (wear loose clothes and drink plenty of fluid).

Pharmacies, identified by the sign "Eczane" or "Eczanesi", are open from 8 a.m. to 8 p.m. The address of an all-night pharmacy will be in the window. Some drugs (even common ones, like certain types of headache tablets) are occasionally in short supply, so if you think you'll be in need of a specific product, bring it with you. You can dial 011 to find out which pharmacy is on duty.

Where's the nearest pharmacy?	**En yakın eczane nerededir?**
Where can I find a doctor/ dentist?	**Neredin bir doktor/bir dişci bulabilirim?**
an ambulance	**bir ambülans**
hospital	**hastane**
sunburn	**güneş yanığı**
sunstroke	**güneş çarptı**
a fever	**ateş**
an upset stomach	**mide bozulması**

HITCH-HIKING
Motorists are willing to give foreigners a ride, but with bus travel so cheap, it's really not worth the bother. Hitch-hiking is not recommended for women on their own.

L LANGUAGE
Turkish is very distantly related to Finnish and Hungarian. It is written in the Roman alphabet, introduced as one of Atatürk's reforms in the 1920s, and is characterized by the use of suffixes to modify meanings, resulting sometimes in amazingly long words.

French used to be the main second language; now it's English, with German-speakers on the increase. Tourist officials and staff in larger hotels speak English. Even people who don't will make a real effort to understand.

The pronunciation of some Turkish letters:
c like **j** in **j**am
ç like **ch** in **ch**ip
ğ silent; lengthens the preceding vowel
h always clearly pronounced
ı like **i** in s**i**r

j like **s** in plea**s**ure
ö approximately like **ur** in f**ur** (like German *ö*)
ş like **sh** in **sh**ell
ü approximately like **ew** in f**ew** (like German *ü*)

If you want to try Turkish, consult the Berlitz phrase book TURK-ISH FOR TRAVELLERS. It covers most situations you're likely to encounter during your Turkish travels.

The following are a few phrases you'll want to use often.

Hello	**Merhaba**	*Goodbye*	**Allahaısmar-**
Good morning	**Günaydın**	*(said by the one*	**ladık**
Good after-noon	**İyi günler**	*who's leaving)*	
		Goodbye	**Güle güle**
Good evening	**İyi akşamlar**	*(said by the one*	
Good night	**İyi geceler**	*who remains)*	

Do you speak English?	**İngilizce biliyor musunuz?**
I don't speak Turkish.	**Türkçe bilmiyorum.**
Yes/No.	**Evet/Hayır.**

MAPS M

The Ministry of Culture and Tourism provides free, useful maps through tourist offices. The maps in this book were prepared by Falk-Verlag, Hamburg, who also publish a map of Istanbul.

MONEY MATTERS

Currency. The monetary unit is the Turkish pound, *lira* (abbr. TL). Coins: 5, 10, 20, 25, 50, 100 TL. Banknotes: 100, 500, 1,000, 5,000 and 10,000 TL.

Banks *(banka)* are open from 8.30 or 9 a.m. to 5 or 5.30 p.m., Monday to Friday, with a lunch break from noon or 12.30 to 1 or 1.30 p.m. Currency can usually be exchanged up to 4 p.m. After hours, money can be exchanged at major hotels. Remember to take your passport for identification, and keep the exchange slips.

Eurocheques, traveller's cheques, credit cards. Eurocheques can be changed at central offices and large branches of major banks. Credit cards are accepted by hotels and establishments used to dealing with visitors. Traveller's cheques can be changed at banks and large hotels. Always present your passport for identification.

The rate should be the same as the Turkish Central Bank rate (published daily in newspapers), although hotels of three-star rating or higher can charge 1% commission.

| I want to change some pounds/ dollars. | Sterlin/Dolar bozdurmak istiyorum. |
| Can I pay with this credit card? | Bu kredi kartımla ödeyebilir miyim? |

N NEWSPAPERS and MAGAZINES

Foreign newspapers and magazines are usually available a day or two after publication. The *Turkish Daily News*, an English-language newspaper published in Ankara, is on sale in cities. The Directorate General of Press and Information publishes a weekly digest, *Newspot*, in Arabic, English, French and German. It is available free of charge from tourist offices.

Stalls at museums and archaeological sites stock publications relating to the areas, often in foreign languages.

| *Have you any English-language newspapers?* | Bir İngiliz gazeteniz var mı? |

P POLICE *(polis)*

A special tourist police section has been set up in Istanbul to help foreigners with problems. The office is in Mimar Kemalettin Caddesi, Sirkeci, tel. 527 45 03. The Tourist Police badge carries the words "Turizm Polisi".

Otherwise, there are the traffic police *(trafik polisi)* in cities and gendarmes *(jandarma)*, a military-run force, in villages where there is no police administration. Military police are recognizable by the letters A.S.İ.Z. on their helmets.

| *Where's the nearest police station?* | En yakın karakol nerede? |

PRICES

To give you an idea of what to expect, here are some average prices in Turkish liras (TL). However, take into account that all prices must be regarded as approximate, and that the inflation rate is high.

Airport transfers. *Istanbul:* taxi to city centre 4,000 TL, bus 550 TL. *Ankara:* taxi, 6,500 TL, bus 550 TL.

Buses. In cities, standard fare 100 TL. Istanbul–Izmir, one way: from 4,000 TL; Edirne–Istanbul: from 500 TL.

Car hire (international company, high season, July–September). *Fiat 124* 14,500 TL per day, 145 TL per km., 39,000 TL per day for 3–6 days' unlimited mileage. *Ford Sierra* 40,800 TL per day, 408 TL per km., 112,000 TL per day for 3–6 days' unlimited mileage. Add 10% tax.

Cigarettes. Turkish brands 300 TL per packet of 20, imported brands 800 L.

Hotels (double room with bath and breakfast). Luxury class 17,000–58,000 TL, 1st class 26,000–33,000 TL, 2nd class 10,000–24,000 TL, 3rd class 4,000–15,000 TL, 4th class 3,500–10,000 TL.

Meals and drinks. Hotel breakfast 1,000–4,000 TL, lunch/dinner in good establishment (table d'hôte) 5,000–8,000 TL, bottle of wine 3,000–5,000 TL, Turkish coffee from 200 TL, small bottle of beer from 400 TL, soft drink (small bottle) from 400 TL.

Museum entry. 100–1,000 TL.

Shoe shine. 100–300 TL.

Turkish bath. From 750 TL.

PUBLIC HOLIDAYS *(milli bayramlar)*

The following are the holidays when banks, schools, offices and shops are closed. The afternoon before a public holiday is often taken off, too.

January 1	*Yılbaşı*	New Year's Day
April 23	*23 Nisan Çocuk Bayramı*	National Independence and Children's Day
May 19	*Gençlik ve Spor Bayramı*	Youth and Sports Day
August 30	*Zafer Bayramı*	Victory Day
October 29	*Cumhuriyet Bayramı*	Republic Day

Apart from these civic celebrations, there are two important Muslim holy periods which are based on the lunar calendar and occur 10 to 22 days earlier each year. The first follows the four weeks daylight fasting and prayer of Ramadan *(Ramazan)* and is called Şeker Bayramı (Sugar Holy Days), lasting three to five days. Two

177

months and ten days later comes the four-to-five day Kurban Bayramı (Holy Days of Sacrifice) festival. During these periods, normal business is interrupted, and you'll find it very difficult to get places on boats and buses or arrange accommodation.

R RESTAURANTS

(See also pp. 156–158.) It helps to know your restaurants in Turkey, for there are several varieties, some of them specializing in specific dishes. A *lokanta* serves Turkish food, but it may also offer a set menu or a "tourist menu" including non-Turkish dishes. *Kebapçı* are experts in grilled meat, especially kebabs served with *pide* bread and rice. Beverages are limited to soft drinks and *ayran* (yoghurt) but you can send out for beer. The Turkish equivalent of a pizza parlour is a *pide salonu*, where flat bread is served hot with meat or cheese and fresh green salad. It makes a good, inexpensive luncheon stop. A *köfteci* specializes in *köfte*, minced lamb croquettes, often garnished with a string-bean salad. Another place for a snack is a *büfe*, which serves sandwiches, hamburgers, sometimes *döner kebap*, toast, cool drinks including yoghurt, but no hot drinks. The *birahane* is a beer-house, where you can buy or send out for accompanying titbits like mussels and shrimps. Wine and *rakı* are also available. Boiled chicken, chicken soup and pilaf are served in a *muhallebici*, as well as local pastries and delicious milk-based desserts, including custards and rice pudding. You will find candies and pastries in a *tatlıcı* and a *pastahane*.

Restaurants usually close at 10 or 11 p.m. for food, in some places even at 9 o'clock.

S SHOPPING and OFFICE HOURS

Government and commercial offices are open from 8.30 a.m. to 12.30 p.m. and from 1.30 to 5.30 p.m., Monday to Friday.

Shops normally open from 9 or 9.30 a.m. to 7 p.m., Monday to Saturday. On the coast, some establishments are closed during the afternoon in the summer, but this doesn't apply to enterprises dealing with tourists. Often, small shops in tourist areas will stay open later, as well as opening on Sundays.

T TIME DIFFERENCES

Turkey follows Eastern European Time, GMT + 2. In summer, clocks are set one hour ahead (GMT + 3), as shown:

New York	London	**Istanbul**	Johannes-burg	Sydney	Auckland
5 a.m.	10 a.m.	**noon**	11 a.m.	7 p.m.	9 p.m.

TIPPING

Service charges are generally included in the bill at hotels and restaurants, but a little extra is usually appreciated, especially for good service. However, tipping can in some cases offend. If the tip is declined forcefully enough, don't insist.

Hotel porter, per bag	150 TL
Maid, per week	1,200 TL
Waiter	5% if service included, 10% if not
Taxi driver	Round up to nearest 200 TL
Tour guide	10% of excursion fare
Hairdresser/Barber	15%

TOILETS

Larger hotels in Turkey have the last word in toilet facilities, down to the paper strip holding seat and lid together that proclaims it has been "Sanitized". Even the toilet paper may be folded so that it hangs decorously. Further down the scale, flushing systems are not fully automatic, in which case the handle should be put back into place (or the tap turned off) to avoid flooding.

Hotels apart, standard procedure is a hole in the ground and twin foot stands, with a paint tin under a dripping tap that can sometimes be coaxed to yield more for flushing purposes. Other thoughtful concessions to communal hygiene might include a rag, and lemon-scented eau de cologne. Most restaurants and filling stations have minimum facilities. Sometimes the door may not lock, but at least that reassures you that you'll be able to get out again. If you can take tissues with you, so much the better.

Where there are separate toilets, men's are marked "Bay(lar)" or "Erkek(ler)", women's "Bayan(lar)" or "Kadın(lar)".

Where are the toilets?   **Tuvaletler nerede?**

TOURIST INFORMATION OFFICES *(turizm danışma bürosu)*

The Turkish Ministry of Culture and Tourism is represented by the Turkish Tourism and Information Office.

Head office:

Gazi Mustafa Kemal Bulvarı 33, Ankara; tel. (4) 229 29 30, ext. 95

Turkish Tourism and Information Offices abroad:

U.K.   170–173 Piccadilly, First Floor, London W1V 9DD; tel. 734 8681

U.S.A.   821 United Nations Plaza, New York, NY 10017; tel. 687-2194

In Turkey, every town of any size has a tourist information office.

Where is the tourist office?	**Turizim bürosu nerede?**

TRANSPORT

Buses *(otobüs)* are cheap but often crowded. For city buses, buy a booklet of tickets, then drop your ticket into the box by the driver. If you don't have a ticket, another passenger will probably help by selling you one. In Istanbul, a *Mavi Kart* (Blue Card) available at main terminals allows you to use the buses for one month from the first day of the month. You need a photo and your passport for identity and will have to wait a day or two to pick the card up.

Taxis *(taksi)* are metered. Have the address written down to avoid struggling to explain directions to drivers, who usually speak only Turkish. In some suburbs of Ankara, there are taxi buttons on lamp posts. At night, you'll be hooted at by one taxi after another; it's their way of indicating that they are free. Tipping is up to you, but since drivers are generally helpful, and the rates are low, you can always add a little.

Dolmuş are shared taxis—a midway solution between taxis and buses. Many official stops are marked with a "D", otherwise wait till a car (usually a big, old American make) slows down, enquire "Dolmuş?" and name your destination. *Dolmuş* run prescribed routes and will let you off where you wish along the way. You're crushed in with other passengers going in the same direction, but it's an inexpensive, efficient system which you can master only through trial and error.

Ferries. Boats leave from Eminönü in old Istanbul for the villages along the Bosphorus and the Golden Horn, and the crossing to Üsküdar on the Asian Coast. For Princes Islands, they set off from Kabataş, early in the morning, then later from Sirkeci. For coastal services and cruises, reserve ahead of time through the Turkish Maritime Lines, which have agents at the quays in all Turkish ports. Izmir has a regular ferry service across the bay to Karşıyaka, which is almost as quick, and more interesting, than a taxi ride.

Long-distance buses. A comprehensive network of buses serves all parts of Turkey. They are cheap, efficient, faster than trains, and comfortable if you take a modern air-conditioned vehicle. Tickets can be bought from agents, but the cheapest will be offered at the bus station *(otogar)* itself. In Istanbul, coaches and minibuses leave from Topkapı Otogarı, the central bus station (not to be confused with Topkapı Palace in quite another area of the city). The station is divided into two sections, the Trakya Otogarı for buses going west and the Anadolu Otogarı for eastbound buses (which also have a terminal at Harem on the Asian side).

Trains. The Turkish State Railways (TCDD) run fast, comfortable trains on *some* major routes. Among the best are the *Mavi Tren* (Blue Train), daily between Istanbul and Ankara (7½ hours), and the *Boğaziçi Ekspresi*, also daily between Istanbul and Ankara (9½ hours, slower than the bus). Stick to trains called *ekspres* or *mototren*, or you may be on them for days. Better still, take a bus.

Istanbul has two railway stations: Sirkeci Garı (Europe) for westbound trains and Haydarpaşa Garı (Asia) for eastbound trains.

Planes. Turkish Airlines (THY) run regular flights connecting Istanbul, Ankara, Izmir and Antalya as well as northern and eastern cities including Trabzon, Erzurum and Van. Flights are reasonably cheap, and THY offer interesting reductions for families, sports groups, students (aged 12 to 26/28) and children on domestic and international departures.

WATER *(su)*   **W**

Tap water is heavily chlorinated, therefore safe to drink but unpleasant in taste. Bottled water, either fizzy (carbonated) or still, is a more agreeable, inexpensive alternative. In smaller restaurants, you may want to follow the example of local people, who rinse the glasses with a little water before drinking.

I'd like a bottle of mineral water.	**Bir şişe maden suyu istiyorum.**
fizzy/still	**soda/su**
drinking water	**su içilir/içilebilir**

WEST AND CENTRAL TURKEY

İnebolu Sinop

0 _____ 100 km
0 _____ 100 miles

N

Kastamonu Boyabat Bafra **Samsun**

...bük Kızılırmak Çarşamba Ordu

Devrez Çayı Merzifon Amasya Erbaa

Kızılırmak Çorum Zile Tokat

Sungurlu ∴Alacahöyük

ANKARA Yazılıkaya Zara

Hattuşaş Boğazkale

Kırıkkale Yozgat Yıldızeli **Sivas**

Hirfanlı Barajı Kızılırmak Kemaliye

Kırşehir

Tuz Gölü Şereflikoçhisar *C a p p a d o c i a*

Göreme Gürün

Nevşehir **Kayseri** Pınarbaşı

Ürgüp Yenice ırmak **Malatya**

Aksaray

Niğde Göksun Adıyaman

Konya Zamantı ırmağı

Çatalhüyük Seyhan N. Kozan Ceyhan (Nehri) **Kahramanmaraş**

Ereğli Fırat N.

Karaman Osmaniye **Gaziantep**

Tarsus Adana Ceyhan Kilis

Mut **Mersin** İskenderun Kırıkhan

Silifke

(MEDITERRANEAN SEA) **Antakya**

183

S Y R I A

KARA DENIZ

(BLACK SEA)

U . S . S . R .

N

Hopa

Trabzon   Rize   Oltu Çay   Kars

Meryemana   Çoruh Nehri   Sarıkamış
(Sumela)

Kelkit Çayı   Aşkal   Pasinler   Horasan   Ağrı   Büyük Ağrı Dağı
                                                                5156
Erzincan   Erzurum
Firat Nehri
Tanyeri   Tutak   Doğubayazıt

Tunceli   Peri Suyu   Murat Nehri   Erciş
Keban   Bingöl
Barajı   Van
Elazığ   Muş   Gölü   Van
                                  Tatvan

Ergani   Silvan   Siirt   Botan Çayı

Nemrut   Diyarbakır   Batman
Dağı
        Dicle Nehri   Şirnak
Siverek   Midyat   Cizre
Firat Nehri
Şanlıurfa   Mardin
          Nusaybin
Altınbaşak   IRAQ

                    Tigris

SYRIA   0   100 km
            0   100 miles

184   EASTERN TURKEY

I R A N

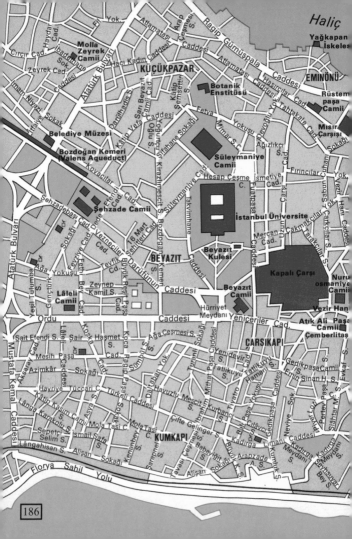

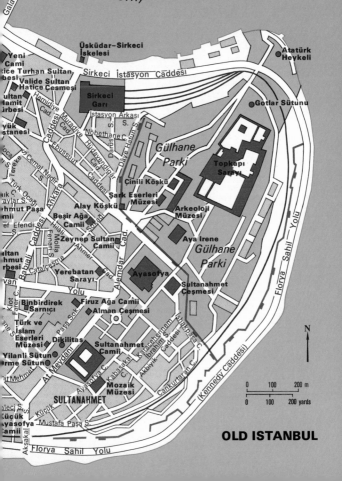

(Golden Horn)

Galata Köprüsü

Üsküdar–Sirkeci
İskelesi

Atatürk
Heykeli

Yeni
Cami
ice Turhan Sultan
besi
Valide Sultan
Hatice Çeşmesi

Sirkeci İstasyon Caddesi

ultan
lamit
irbesi

Hamidiye
Cad.

Sirkeci
Garı

Gotlar Sütunu

yük
stanesi

İstasyon Arkası

Muradiye Cad.

Hüdavendigar Cad.

Nöbethane C.

Danış Tahin S.

Gülhane
Parki

Topkapı
Sarayı

oca
2 Cemal Nadir

Ebussuut
Caddesi

Ankara

Çinili Köşkü

Şark Eserleri
Müzesi

ık S.
Terece
S.

Türk Ocağı
ıylar S.
hmut Paşa
mii
ef Efendi
S.

Alay Köşkü

Hilali Molla
Fenari S.

Beşir Ağa
Camii

Zeynep Sultan
Camii

Ahmet

Arkeoloji
Müzesi

Aya İrene

Gülhane
Parki

ultan
hmut
rbesi

Babıali
Çatalçeşme

Alemdar Cad.

Ayasofya

Caddesi

Yerebatan
Sarayı

Sultanahmet
Çeşmesi

Florya Sahil Yolu

van

Klot
arer S.

Binbirdirek
Sarnıcı

Firuz Ağa Camii

Alman Çeşmesi

Paşa Sok.

Türk ve
İslam
Eserleri
Müzesi

Dikilitaş

Yilanli Sütun
rme Sütun

At Meydanı

Sultanahmet
Camii

Kaşıkçıhan
İbrahim

Akbıyık Caddesi

Cankurtaran C.

(Kennedy Caddesi)

hit Mehmet

Ayasofya C.

Kabasakal

Mozaik
Müzesi

SULTANAHMET

aleci S.

Küçük
yasofya
amii

Mustafa Paşa S.

Aksakal

Florya Sahil Yolu

N

0   100   200 m

0   100   200 yards

OLD ISTANBUL

INDEX

An asterisk (*) next to a page number indicates a map reference. Where there is more than one set of page references, the one in bold type refers to the main entry. For index to Practical Information, see pp. 160-161.

Adana 15, 183*
Adıyaman 140, 183*
Aegean Coast 73-88, 182*
Aksaray 124, 183*
Alanya 6*, 102-104, 182*
Alexander the Great 19, 22, 30, 75, 96
Anamur 6*, 104
Ankara 6*, 10, 15, 33, 34, 107, **108-114**, 183*, 188*
  Anıt Kabir 109, 188*
  Atatürk Köşkü 111
  Augustus Mabedi 108
  Hisar (Kale) 109, 188*
  Julianus Sütunu 108, 188*
  Mosques (Cami)
    Arslanhane 109, 188*
    Hacı Bayram 108, 188*
    Kocatepe 112, 188*
  Museums (Müze)
    Anadolu Medeniyetleri 112, 115, 128, 188*
    Atatürk 111
    Etnografya 112, 188*
  Roma Hamamı 108, 188*
  Ulus Meydanı 108, 188*
Antalya 6*, 34, 94, **96-98**, 101, 102, 155, 182*
Aphrodisias 6*, 84, 182*
Ararat, Mt. (Ağrı Dağı) 7*, 15, **144-145**, 184*

Aspendos 6*, 99, 182*
Atatürk, Mustafa Kemal 12, 31, 41, 59, 108, 109, 111, 129, 130, 134, 139
Avanos 120
Aydin 155, 182*
Ayvalık 6*, 69, 182*

Black Sea Coast 129-136
Bodrum 6*, 85, **86-88**, 147, 152, 155, 182*
Boğazköy-Hattuşaş 6*, 17, 107, **114-117**, 183*
Bursa 6*, 15, 36, **65-66**, 68, 148, 150, 152, 155, 182*

Camel wrestling 149
Cappadocia 33, 107, **117-124**, 155, 183*
Caunus 91
Central Anatolia 107-128
Claros 77
Colophon 77
Constantine 22, 38, 42, 47

Çanakkale 6*, 68, 73, 155, 182*
Çatalhüyük 6*, 10, 30, 107, 114, 126, **128**, 183*
Çeşme 6*, 73, **78-79**, 182*
Çorum 155

189

Datça 6*, 89, 147, 182*
Dalyan 91
Demre (Myra) 6*, **92–93**, 155, 182*
Derinkuyu 123
Didyma (Didim) 85, 182*
Dikili 69
Diyarbakır 155, 184*
Doğubayazıt 144, 145, 184*

Eastern Turkey 136–146
Eating out 156–158
Edirne 6*, 26, 36, **69–72**, 149, 155, 182*
Entertainment 153–155
Ephesus (Efes) 6*, 10, 21, 74, **81–84**, 182*
Erzurum 7*, 34, 136, **137–140**, 149, 184*
Eski Foça 74

Fethiye 6*, **91**, 147, 182*

Gallipoli (Gelibolu) 6*, 27, 36, 69, **73**, 182*
Gemile 91
Giresun 129, **132**
Göreme 6*, 118, **120**, 183*

Hatti people 16
Hattuşaş, see Boğazköy
Heaven and Hell Caves (Cennet ve Cehennem) 106
Hittites 10, 16, 33, 112

Ihlara 124
Ishak Paşa Sarayı 145
Istanbul 6*, 9, 15, 33, **35–62**, 68, 69, 147, 149, 150, 152, 154, 155, 182*, 185*, 186–187*
  Anadolu Hisarı 36, 61, 63
  Anadolu Kavagı 64
  At Meydanı 37, **38**, 42, 187*

Aya İrini Kilisesi 43, **46**, 187*
Beyazıt Meydanı 47
Beylerbeyi Palace 36, 61, 63
Bosphorus Bridge 61, 63
Bozdoğan Kemeri 50, 186*
Cirağan Palace 62
Çamlıca Park 36, 61
Çemberlitas 47, 186*
Çiçek Pasajı 58
Çukurbostan 51
Dolmabahçe Sarayı 36, **59**, 62, 185*
Edirnekapı 54
Eminönü 54, 186*
Eyüp 36, **64**
Galata 56, 185*
Galata Bridge 37, 50, 54, **56**, 187*
Golden Horn 64, 185*, 186–187*
Grand Bazaar, see Kapalı Çarşı
Hippodrome, see At Meydanı
İstiklâl Caddesi 58, 185*
Karacaahmet 61
Leander's Tower 37
Markets (Çarşı)
  Kapalı 48–49, 186*
  Mısır 54, 186*
  Sahaflar 49
Mosques (Cami)
  Beyazıt 47, 186*
  Blue, see Sultan Ahmet
  Eyüp Sultan 64
  Fatih 51
  Fethiye 51
  İskele 62
  Kariye 50, **52**
  Kiliç Ali Paşa 58, **62**
  Küçük Ayasofya 39, 187*
  Mehmet Paşa 39
  Mihrimah 53
  Molla Çelebi 62

Istanbul (contd.)
  Nuruosmaniye 47, 186*
  Rüstempaşa 56, 186*
  Sülemaniye 37, 49-50, 186*
  Sultan Ahmet 37, 38, 39, 187*
  Sultan Selim 51
  Şehzade 50
  Yeni 37, 54, 187*
  Yeni Valide 62
  Museums (Müze)
    Arkeoloji 46, 187*
    Askeri 59, 185*
    Ayasofya 24, 26, 39, 133, 187*
    Çinili Köşkü 47, 187*
    Deniz 60
    Eski Şark Eserleri 47, 187*
    Resim ve Heykel 60
    St. Sophia, see Ayasofya
    Türk ve İslam Eserleri 38, 187*
  Pera Palas 58, 185*
  Rumeli Hisarı 36, 60, 61, 64
  Rumeli Kavağı 64
  Selimiye Kişlası 62
  Sultanahmet district 38, 197*
  Taksim Meydanı 58, 185*
  Tefkur Sarayı 54
  Theodosian Walls 54
  Topkapı Sarayı 37, 42-46, 51, 187*
  Üsküdar 61
  Valens Aqueduct, see Bozdoğan Kemeri
  Yedikule 54
  Yerebatan Sarayı 42, 187*
  Yıldız Park 36, 60
  Yıldız Sarayı 60
Izmir 6*, 15, 18, 21, 33, 68, 74-76, 84, 149, 155, 182*
Iznik 152

Janissaries 27, 42, 46, 59
Justinian the Great 24, 41, 42, 46, 135

Kale 92
Kalkan 92
Kaputaş 92
Kaş 6*, 92, 147, 182*
Kaymaklı 120
Kekova 92
Kemal, Mustafa, see Atatürk
Keykubat, Alaettin 96, 103, 124, 126, 137
Kilyos 64, 147
Kirşehir 155
Kızkalesi 106
Knidos 88
Konya 6*, 33, 106, 107, 124-128, 155, 183*
Kos 74, 88, 182*
Küçük Kargı 91
Kuşadası 6*, 79-80, 84, 85, 147, 152, 182*

Loti, Pierre 64

Malatya 140, 183*
Malazgirt 142
Mamure Kilesi 104
Manavgat 6*, 101-102, 182*
Manisa 6*, 77, 155, 182*
Marmaris 6*, 88, 89, 91, 147, 152, 155, 182*
Mediterranean Coast 89-107
Mehmet the Conquerer (Fatih) 12, 25, 26, 41, 42, 44, 47, 49, 51, 54, 133
Mersin 6*, 107, 155, 183*
Mevlana (Celaleddin Rumi) 124, 125
Miletus (Milet) 85, 182*
Myra, see Demre

191

INDEX

Nemrut Dağı 7*, 140–142, 184*
Nevşehir 6*, 107, **118**, 183*
Noah's Ark 145

Oil wrestling 149
Olympos 94–95
Ordu 7*, 131

Ölü Deniz 91

Palandöken Tesisleri 139
Pamukkale 6*, **84**, 152, 182*
Patara 92
Pergamum (Bergama) 6*, 21, **73–74**, 152, 155, 182*
Perge 6*, 96, **99**, 101, 182*
Phaselis 95
Pontus, Kingdom of 21, 129, 135
Priene 85, 182*
Princes Islands 36, **65**, 147

Rhodes 6*, 89, 182*
Rize 7*, 129, 184*

St. Nicholas 92, 94, 98
St. Paul 10, 106, 107, 124
St. Thecla 106
Samsun 7*, 111, **129–130**, 183*
Sardis (Sart) 6*, 21, **76**, 182*
Schliemann, Heinrich 68
Selçuk 6*, 81, **84**, 149, 155, 182*
Side 6*, 102, 182*
Silifke 6*, 106, 183*
Sinan 26, 41, 46, 49, 50, 53, 62, 69, 139
Sinop 6*, 129, 183*
Smyrna, see Izmir

Softa Kalesi 105
Soğanlı 118, **120–124**
Sports 147–149
Suleiman the Magnificent 26, 31, 134
Sumela Monastery (Meryemana) 134, 184*

Şile 64, 147
Şövalye 91

Tarabya 64, 156
Tarsus 6*, 107, 183
Tatvan 7*, 142, 184*
Teos 77
Termessos 6*, 98–99, 182*
Thrace 9, 15, **69–72**
Tirebolu 132
Trabzon 7*, 33, 111, 129, **132–134**, 184*
Troy (Truva) 6*, 10, 18, 36, **68–69**, 182*

Uçhisar 120
Ürgüp 6*, 118, 183

Van 7*, 34, **142–144**, 184*

Xanthos 6*, 91, 182*

Yalova 6*, 65, 182*
Yanar 95
Yazılıkaya 115, **116**
Yeni Foça 74
Young Turks 27

Zelve 120

028/808 RP